D1528195

INDIAN
PATRIOTS
Of The
EASTERN
WOODLANDS

A TARGET BOOK

INDIAN PATRIOTS
Of The
EASTERN
WOODLANDS

Edited, with commentary by Bennett Wayne

GARRARD PUBLISHING COMPANY
CHAMPAIGN, ILLINOIS

Picture credits:

The Bettmann Archive: pp. 15, 36, 43, 149, cover
Carnegie Library, Pittsburgh: p. 57
Culver Pictures: pp. 30, 101, 142
Delaware Art Museum, Wilmington, Delaware: p. 6
Field Museum of Natural History, Chicago: p. 48
Gilcrease Institute of American History and Art,
    Tulsa, Oklahoma: p. 128
Library of Congress: p. 94
National Collection of Fine Arts, Smithsonian Institution:
    pp. 66, 84, 106 (all), 114 (all), 115 (both), 132
New York Public Library, Picture Collection: pp. 69, 78, 81, 136
Courtesy Frederick John Pratson: p. 8
The St. Louis Art Museum: p. 124
University of Miami Library, Coral Gables, Florida: p. 160

Acknowledgments:

The quotations on the following pages are from the
sources listed:
Page 9: Winslow, Edward and Bradford, William.
    Mourt's Relations. London, 1622.
Page 49: Josephy, Alvin M., Jr. *The Patriot Chiefs.*
    New York, Viking Press, 1961.
Page 85: Jackson, Donald, ed. *Black Hawk*. Urbana,
    Illinois, The University of Illinois Press, 1955.
Page 133: Tebbel, John. *The Compact History of the Indian
    Wars*. New York, Hawthorn Books, 1966.

Library of Congress Cataloging in Publication Data

Wayne, Bennett.
    Indian patriots of the eastern woodlands.

    (Target)
    Includes index.
    SUMMARY: Brief biographies of four Indian chiefs:
Massasoit, Tecumseh, Black Hawk, and Osceola.

    1. Indians of North America—Biography—Juvenile
literature. [1. Indians of North America—
Biography] I. Title.
E89.W38   973′.04′97 [B] [920]   75-20048
ISBN 0-8116-4916-4

Contents

The First Americans

They were the first Americans—the first to live on the land, the first to cultivate it. They were the Indians of Eastern America—Wampanoag, Shawnee, Sauk and Fox, Seminole, and hundreds of others.

In the beginning the Indians welcomed their white brothers and taught them how to survive in the wilderness. And they gave generously of their fields and forests. But soon the white men filled every corner of the land and demanded still more. By treaty, and then by force, the Indians were driven from their homes and across the Mississippi to a harsh new life.

Some few tribes, some few Indian leaders stayed on and fought for their homes, their hunting grounds, and their people's right to remain where the bones of their ancestors were buried. This book is about a few of these Indian patriots.

Massasoit was one of the very first to welcome his white brothers and to pledge his friendship forever. He lived to regret his generosity. Tecumseh tried to unite all of the tribes into a mighty Indian nation with the strength to fight the white invaders and win back Indian lands. Black Hawk refused to leave his native village until the bitter end. His trail northward in search of food became a trail of blood and tears. Osceola's battle to keep his people in the Florida wilderness was doomed, but he fought on in the fiercest Indian war of all.

Brave men and women on both sides died in the struggle. In the end even those Indians who had vowed to fight to the death were forced to surrender. And a proud people, as Tecumseh had predicted, was "scattered as autumnal leaves before the wind."

Massasoit

Friend of the Pilgrims

by Virginia Voight

We have found the Indians very faithful in their covenant of peace with us, very loving and ready to pleasure us . . . not only the greatest king amongst them, called Massasoyt, but also all the princes and peoples round about us. . . . We, for our part, walk as peaceably and safely in the wood as in the highways in England.

From Mourt's Relations *by Edward Winslow and William Bradford (London, 1622)*

9

1. A Boy of the Wampanoag Tribe

Before dawn the Wampanoag village was already stirring. This was long before the first white settlers came to New England.

Yellow Feather, the son of the head chief, stood in the doorway of the wigwam. He had been awakened by a Wampanoag war cry, a wild sound, like the scream of an angry eagle. It meant that a party of Wampanoag braves was about to leave the village and go on the warpath.

The boy's heart beat faster as he watched his father lead the painted warriors through a gate in the village stockade. They were grim and silent as they passed out of sight into the dark forest.

Yellow Feather's baby brother Quadequina, propped in his cradleboard against the wall of the wigwam, made a sleepy little sound. Their mother, the Wampanoag *saunk*, or queen, came swiftly into the wigwam.

"Mother, are the Narragansett raiding us again?" Yellow Feather asked.

His mother nodded. "A runner brought word that a war party has burned a Wampanoag vil-

lage. Your father has gone to drive the enemy
away."

Yellow Feather's eyes flashed. He wished that
he were old enough to put on war paint and
help his father defend their tribal lands against
the Narragansett.

The Narragansett tribe lived on the west side of
Narragansett Bay. The country of the Wampanoag
was to the east and north of the bay. As long as
anyone could remember, the two tribes had been
at war. Warriors of both tribes went raiding into
the country of the enemy. They would burn villages and take captives. Then they would return to
their own country and tell of their adventures in
songs and dances. To Yellow Feather, war cries
and the whiz of arrows were an ordinary part of
life. The same was true for the children across the
border in Narragansett country.

Yellow Feather's mother moved about the wigwam, rolling up fur robes and packing food in
carrying baskets. If the Narragansett reached this
village, the Wampanoag women and children
would flee into the cedar swamps to hide.

Yellow Feather took down his small bow and
quiver of arrows from where they hung on the
wall.

"I will defend you and Quadequina if we are
attacked by the Narragansett," he told his mother.

He took his bow and stood guard outside the stockade with an old man of the tribe. At last, almost at dusk, he heard voices far down the trail. The Wampanoag war party was returning, and Yellow Feather knew that his people had won the battle. The people who were coming could not be Narragansett. A war party on the way to attack a village moved as softly as a forest cat. With a cry of joy he ran to the stockade gate.

"*Hio!*" he shouted. "Our warriors are home again!"

That night the happy Wampanoag people gathered in the village dancing place. Drums filled the air with a deep-toned beat, while the warriors leaped and stamped in a victory dance. All the people clapped their hands and chanted in time with the drums.

Off to one side Yellow Feather pranced about, shaking two turtle-shell rattles in a victory dance of his own. The other village boys fell in behind him, bending low and leaping high as they copied the dance steps of their fathers. As the boys danced, Yellow Feather sang:

> *Hio! The Narragansett came creeping.*
> *To Wampanoag country came they*
> *to burn and slay.*
> *My father and his braves met them*
> *with war clubs.*

Wampanoag arrows sang and bit!
The Narragansett ran howling back
* to their own land.*
Tonight, Narragansett villages are dark.
The air is filled with moaning.
Victory! Victory to the Wampanoag!

2. How Yellow Feather Got His Name

Yellow Feather was the oldest son of the Wampanoag *sachem*, or head chief. He tried very hard to be the leader in games and shooting contests with the other boys. He stood tall for his age and would no doubt be a powerful man.

The other boys accepted him as their leader because he was strong and fearless. He was also generous, warmhearted, and likable. His mother and father thought proudly that he was born to be a great chief. His mother was sure that she knew the reason.

A few days before Yellow Feather was born, the saunk had gone into the forest to pray. She prayed to Kiehtan the Great Spirit. She asked the Great Spirit to give her a son. And she prayed that her baby might grow up to be a brave leader.

Suddenly the shadow of wings swept over her. She looked up to see a flicker pass overhead. As she watched, a yellow feather dropped from one of

13

the bird's wings and fell glistening at her feet. The saunk gave a happy cry. Surely Kiehtan had sent the flicker as a sign that her prayer would be answered!

Several nights later her son was born. She named him Ousamequin, or Yellow Feather.

3. Yellow Feather and the Bear

In late February, when the days are warm and nights are cold, sap rises in the maple trees. This was the time for the Wampanoag women to make maple syrup and maple sugar. The year that Yellow Feather was twelve, his mother sent Quadequina around to all the wigwams in the Wampanoag winter village. She said to tell the women that it was time to start for the maple grove.

The next morning a group of women, girls, and boys started out on snowshoes for the nearest grove. Yellow Feather and the older boys walked first. They were armed with bows and arrows in case the party met a pack of hungry wolves.

The women and younger children pulled sleds loaded with rolled sleeping robes, cooking pots, and other gear. The maple grove was a long walk through the woods in deep snow, so the party would camp there until the run of sap was over.

Some of the boys used their snowshoes to clear a
space for the camp. Some caught rabbits and shot
squirrels for supper. Others helped their mothers
make shelters of poles and evergreen branches, and
break up dead wood for fires. Soon clay pots of
rich stew were bubbling over the fires.

Under the direction of the saunk, a deep gash
was cut in the trunk of each maple, tree. Sap ran
out and dripped into troughs made of birch bark
that had been set beneath the cuts.

Yellow Feather saw a porcupine on the trunk of
a maple tree. The porcupine was licking hungrily
at a trickle of sap. All of the children gathered

Yellow Feather helped set up camps much like
this one, where maple sap was collected.

around to watch him, but no one tried to chase him away. The Indians thought that this forest neighbor had as much right to the maple sap as they did.

When the troughs were full, the children emptied the sap into clay pots that were set on the hot coals of the fires to boil. From time to time the women tested the boiling syrup by dropping some from their long wooden stirring paddles onto the snow. When it cooled and became hard, the children popped the chewy candy into their mouths.

"Let us dance to thank the forest spirits for their gift of sweetness," Yellow Feather called out to his friends.

He began to stamp in and out among the trees of the maple grove. The other children fell in behind him and began to chant a song:

> *Thanks to you, O Maple Spirit.*
> *You made the sap run thick and sweet!*
> *Thanks to you, O Fire Spirit.*
> *You boiled the pots and helped the*
>   *sugar come.*

An angry roar at the edge of the grove cut short the song. The children froze. The women looked up in alarm. The older boys readied their bows. Everyone peered to see what had made the noise.

A black bear had been hibernating in an old hollow tree at the edge of the grove. In their dance the children had come close to the tree, and their singing had awakened him. He growled angrily and crawled out of the tree. He was huge and frightening. The breeze brought him the smell of maple syrup and made him hungry. *Roarrrr!* His big furry body plowed through the snow toward them.

Yellow Feather gathered all the children together and stood between them and the bear. Indians had a great respect for bears. Usually several men would go together on a bear hunt. Today there were only boys to protect the women and girls.

The boys didn't want to shoot the bear. Unless they made an especially lucky shot, it would take a number of arrows to kill him. In his pain and fury he might kill or hurt several Indians.

Yellow Feather raised his hand. "Peace to you, Mooin!"

Mooin didn't want peace. The bear ran to a pot that had just been lifted off the fire. He slapped at the pot with his paw and turned it over. Then he roared as the hot syrup burned his paws.

"Go away, Mooin!" cried the saunk, waving her stirring paddle.

The bear swung his great head around to look at her. He thought the saunk had caused his pain.

Snarling, he reared up on his hind legs. His long teeth gleamed in his open jaws.

Yellow Feather stepped between his mother and the bear. He quickly shot an arrow from his bow. It struck the bear in the chest and angered him even more. He ran at Yellow Feather. Yellow Feather hit him with another arrow and then pulled out his flint knife. The bear had come too close now for shooting.

Yellow Feather struck with his knife just as the bear swung his huge paw and knocked the boy down. Then Yellow Feather felt a crushing blow as Mooin fell across him.

The saunk ran up, followed by the others. Mooin was dead. It took the combined strength of all the women and boys to roll his huge bulk off Yellow Feather. As they rolled the bear free of him, Yellow Feather gave a broken gasp.

"He lives! Yellow Feather lives!" shouted his friends.

Yellow Feather sat up. He was breathing hard. Blood ran from the long cuts made by the bear's claws. Before he would let the women tend to his wounds, he must make his peace with the spirit of the bear. He lifted one hand in salute, as to a brave warrior.

"Forgive me, Mooin," he pleaded. "I had to kill you."

Later, the saunk made Yellow Feather a necklace of the bear's claws. Only the best hunters of the tribe had ever won such a necklace. The sachem held a grand feast to celebrate his son's courage.

Now the Wampanoag gave Yellow Feather a new name. They called the boy Massasoit, which means the "Brave One," or the "Great One."

4. The White Captives

Ten years and more passed. Massasoit was grown now, and a leader of the young men of the tribe.

In most of the New England tribes the oldest son of a sachem became chief when his father died. Massasoit was still a young man when he became chief.

In wars with the Narragansett and other tribes, the new sachem had already proved himself to be a bold leader. He now showed his people that he was also great in the ways of peace. He got many small tribes to form a union with the Wampanoag. In this way he became grand sachem, or head chief, over a vast territory. Wampanoag country now included most of what is now southern Massachusetts, some of Rhode Island, Cape Cod, and a number of offshore islands.

One day a band of Massachusetts came to see Massasoit in his village, Sowams, at the head of Narragansett Bay. They were dragging two dirty, ragged white men. The captives had cuts and bruises that showed that they had been roughly treated.

Massasoit and his friend Hobomok were smoking their pipes under a great oak tree close to the sachem's wigwam. The sachem invited the Massachusetts chief to join them. His youngest wife brought a pouch of tobacco and filled the visitor's pipe.

They smoked a few minutes in silence. Then the Massachusetts chief said to Massasoit, "Great chief, I bring you these white slaves as a gift."

Massasoit looked at the scowling captives. He had seen white men before, but never so close. Sometimes French or English ships sailed along the coast to fish and trade with the Indians. From lookouts at the edge of the forest, Massasoit had watched them pass. He did not like white men. Years before, an English sea captain had kidnapped some Wampanoag Indians near Patuxet, a coastal village. The Englishman had taken these Wampanoag far away to a place called Europe and sold them as slaves.

"Where do these white captives come from?" the sachem asked.

"From a far-off nation called France," the Massachusetts chief told him. "A French captain put into Massachusetts Bay in his big canoe. He wanted to trade for beaver skins. But he cheated our people and killed one of us." The chief paused for a moment and then went on. "One night we went out to the French canoe in our dugouts. We killed all the French except this many." He held up six fingers. "We made them slaves and burned their canoe. These are for you, great sachem."

Massasoit nodded his thanks. "I accept the gift." He spoke to the saunk, who was seated nearby. "Wife, put these slaves to work."

One of the six French slaves had had smallpox when he was taken prisoner by the Massachusetts. The Indians had never heard about this terrible sickness. The man died, and soon the other French prisoners came down with smallpox. The Indians, too, became ill with it.

The clean, healthy bodies of the Indians of the New World could not fight against the many kinds of sickness of the white men. Hundreds of New England Indians became ill with smallpox and died. The Indians who were left could not bury them all. For years the bones and skulls of those who had died lay white upon the ground.

Massasoit lost many of his people in the great sickness, but his French slaves did not die. It angered the sachem to see them going about their work. He wondered if he should kill them. Had not their fellows brought death to many Indians?

Before he had made up his mind, two visitors arrived at Sowams. One was Samoset, a chief of the Pemaquid tribe in Maine. Samoset liked to travel, and he had visited Massasoit before. The other Indian was a Wampanoag named Squanto.

Massasoit was surprised to see Squanto for he was one of the Indians who had been kidnapped from Patuxet.

"How did you get here, Squanto?" he asked. "How did you escape from your captors?"

"It is a very long story, great sachem. Captain Dermer, an English sea captain, brought me home to my own land. He is a good man."

Massasoit looked at Squanto with pity. "Alas, all your people died in the great sickness."

Squanto nodded sadly. "Captain Dermer landed at Patuxet. We saw the bones of my people in the fields."

"You are welcome now to make your home at Sowams," Massasoit told him.

"Thank you, great sachem," Squanto said. Then he added, "Today I bring a message from Captain Dermer. He sends you gifts, and he wishes to ask a favor of you."

"What is it?" Massasoit asked.

Squanto looked uneasy. He was afraid that what Captain Dermer asked might make the head chief angry.

"The captain has heard that you hold two white men captive. He begs you to give them up to him."

The sachem thought while he stared into the distance. Perhaps this was the best way to get rid of the slaves. Finally Massasoit nodded. "Tell the captain that he may have them."

Squanto and Samoset remained at Sowams after Captain Dermer had sailed away with the two French captives.

5. The English Come to Patuxet

About six months later some Wampanoag scouts brought exciting news to Sowams. There were white people living at Patuxet! As the English reckoned time, this was in the winter of 1620–1621.

The news made Massasoit angry. More white people! Had they come with a new sickness, or to kidnap more Indians? Perhaps he should lead a war party to Patuxet and kill them!

He sent the scouts back to Patuxet to keep watch on the strangers.

After a few days the scouts came back. They told Massasoit that the strangers were going to stay. They were building a new village, which they called Plymouth.

"They have brought their women and their children, and they are cutting down trees and building wigwams."

"These strangers do not know how to act in the woods," the second scout said. "Some of their men went hunting and followed a trail where we had set a trap for deer. One stranger, called Bradford by the others, stepped into our trap. It jerked him into the air—"

The two scouts slapped themselves and roared with laughter at the thought of Bradford dangling from a tree by one foot.

"Friends cut Bradford down," the scout added.

Then he stopped laughing as he remembered something else he had seen at Patuxet. "On top of the hill above their village," he told Massasoit, "the strangers have built a fort. In this fort is the biggest firestick ever seen."

The scouts' words made Massasoit thoughtful. The Indians knew little about guns and did not own any. They had seen only those of the few white traders who had landed on their coast. Massasoit had never heard of a cannon like the one at the fort at Patuxet. He and his people believed that white men used magic to store great thunder and lightning in their "firesticks."

An Indian watches as the Pilgrims land at Plymouth.

"The war chief at Patuxet must have an extra large supply of lightning in that big firestick," Massasoit said. "Such a man would be a powerful ally in our wars with the Narragansett."

Samoset was still visiting at Sowams. He had been friendly with English sailors who fished along the Maine coast and had learned to speak some English from them. One day in early spring, Massasoit asked Samoset to go to Patuxet and talk with the white men.

"My scouts will wait in the woods to help you, if the strangers should prove unfriendly."

"I am not afraid of the strangers," Samoset said proudly and started on his long walk.

Massasoit could hardly wait to hear more about the white people at Patuxet. Should he make friends with them, or should he drive them away? Their fate would depend upon Samoset's report.

Within a few days Samoset was back at Sowams. He told Massasoit that he had walked into the village at Patuxet shouting, "Welcome, Englishmen!"

"The strangers seemed glad to see me," Samoset said. "They took me to their head men, who welcomed me and gave me English food. I told them that I brought greetings from Massasoit, the greatest chief in all this land. Then, great sachem," Samoset went on, "the English chief, whose name is Governor Carver, asked me to invite you to visit him. The English are eager to make friends with you."

After thinking over all that Samoset had told him, Massasoit decided to go to Patuxet. He took 60 warriors with him, including his brother Quadequina, Hobomok, Samoset, and Squanto. Squanto spoke English better than Samoset, and he would be Massasoit's "tongue" in talking to the strangers.

Massasoit stopped his party in the woods near Patuxet. "Go tell the strangers that I am here!" he ordered Samoset and Squanto.

Word that the great chief had arrived with 60 warriors caused excitement and fear in Plymouth. Captain Miles Standish ordered the twelve men in his army to put on their armor and shoulder their muskets. The people rushed into the street and stared wide-eyed at the hill across the brook. The sight of Massasoit and his warriors filled them with awe.

At this time Massasoit was in the prime years of his life. He was a magnificent looking man, and he carried himself with royal dignity. He had rubbed his tall body with walnut oil. It shone like bronze. He had painted his face a mulberry red. Anyone who saw him would know he was a powerful and important man.

He wore moccasins and fringed leggings of deerskin. The leggings were tied to a belt that held up his breechclout. Fastened over one shoulder was a robe of doeskin. It looked almost as soft as white satin. At the edge of this robe there was a design made of colored porcupine quills and moose hair. Around his neck was a necklace of bone beads, a braided cord from which hung a great knife of chipped stone in a leather cover, and a tobacco pouch. In his hair he wore an eagle feather to mark his rank.

Quadequina, Hobomok, and all the other warriors were enormous men. They had painted their faces in streaks and stars of red, black, and white. All the Indians looked impressive enough to make the Pilgrims gasp.

Young Edward Winslow went to meet and to welcome the visiting sachem. He made a courtly bow to Massasoit and gave him presents from Governor Carver. The pair of English knives and the copper necklace set with a sparkling jewel pleased Massasoit.

"Tell this Englishman that I will go at once to meet his governor," he said to Squanto.

Massasoit still remembered the kidnapping, however, and he did not entirely trust these strangers.

"The Englishman must remain here with Quadequina until I come back," he said. To show that he meant no harm to the people at

Patuxet he added, "I and my braves will leave our weapons here when we enter the village."

Hobomok, Samoset, Squanto, and four other warriors went with Massasoit as he walked down the hill. Captain Standish and his red-coated men were waiting at the brook to form an honor guard. Massasoit towered above the short, sturdy captain as they walked along Plymouth Street side by side.

At the head of the group marched a small military band. The shrilling of the fifes, the rolling of the drum, and the clear notes of the trumpet delighted Massasoit and his Indians. Using sign language, one warrior got the trumpeter to let him play his instrument. He took the trumpet and blew into it with all his might. Only a dismal squawking sound came out. The other Indians thought that this was very funny, but the Pilgrims were afraid to laugh.

Pilgrim women and children stood on either side of the road to see Massasoit go by. Some of the children cheered; others stared in wide-eyed silence.

Massasoit looked about him with wonder. He was enjoying this visit. An empty house had been made ready for his coming. As he entered, he looked around the room. He liked the green carpet that covered the floor, and the green cushions which were arranged to serve as seats.

Massasoit is greeted by Miles Standish and a
military band on his visit to Plymouth.

The sachem and the governor sat down facing
each other. Several Pilgrim women hurried in with
platters of carefully prepared food. Massasoit tasted
each dish and then handed it to his followers to
enjoy.

With Squanto speaking the words after him in
the Wampanoag tongue, Governor Carver gave
Massasoit a message from King James. He said that
the king would like to have Massasoit for his
friend and ally. He asked the sachem to give the
land at Patuxet to the English and to make a
treaty of peace that would help both Indians and
Pilgrims.

Massasoit had been quietly studying the Pilgrims. He decided that these were honest, trustworthy people.

"The Wampanoag come to their white brothers with open hands and hearts," he said. "Let there never be a warpath between us. Yes, Englishmen, take this land," he added sadly. "There is only one Patuxet left."

He took his carved stone pipe and some tobacco from his deerskin pouch. Samoset brought a coal to light the pipe. Massasoit took a deep puff and passed the pipe to Governor Carver.

"It is an Indian custom to honor a treaty," Samoset explained.

As Massasoit and the governor smoked together, a feeling of trust and friendship filled the little house.

6. Friends and Neighbors

When Massasoit returned to Sowams, he said that Squanto could remain at Plymouth. Squanto would act as the "tongue" of both Indians and Pilgrims while they were learning each other's language.

Other Wampanoag came to Plymouth to visit for a few days and to enjoy the English food. When one left, another would soon appear. The Pilgrims worried because their Indian visitors were eating up so much of their small supply of food. They worried also because so few Indians brought furs to trade. Finally Governor Carver sent Edward Winslow to Sowams. He was to ask Massasoit to allow only those Indians with furs to trade to go to Plymouth.

With Squanto to guide him, Winslow hiked the long woodland trail to Sowams. They found the village almost empty. Massasoit had gone with most of his people to a seaside camp to feast on clams and lobsters.

Squanto asked an Indian runner to go to Massasoit and to tell him that he had visitors. The sachem returned at once to Sowams. He was glad to see Edward Winslow, and yet unhappy because there was no food in his wigwam to offer his guests. He himself went out on Narragansett Bay in his canoe and caught two large sea bass for dinner. Afterward, when he and Winslow had time to talk, Massasoit said that he was sorry to hear that the Pilgrims had been feeding so many uninvited Indians. He promised that his people would not go to Plymouth so often.

"But let the hunters bring us furs to trade," Winslow begged.

"The hunters will come," Massasoit promised.

To make this clear, he asked his people to

gather in the dancing place. The sachem stood before his wigwam with his arms folded on his broad chest. Later, in a book called *Good Newes From New-England*, Edward Winslow set down as much as he could understand of the sachem's speech.

"Am I not the head chief of this country?" Massasoit roared.

"*Wah!*" an answering cry went up from the people.

"And if I tell Wampanoag hunters to carry their fur to Patuxet, will they not go there?" Massasoit asked.

"*Wah!*" yelled the Indians. "They will go to Patuxet!"

"And will not my anger be terrible if they do not go?"

"*Wah!* It will be terrible!" they shouted.

These questions and answers flew back and forth for so long that Edward Winslow grew tired, although he dared not let the sachem know this. He was happy, however, that the Wampanoag hunters would now trade their furs at Plymouth.

When Winslow and Squanto went back to Plymouth, Massasoit's friend Hobomok went with them. Hobomok would now live at Plymouth most of the time. He would act for Massasoit in any business that might come up with the Pilgrims.

Hobomok was an important man among the Indians, known for his courage and wisdom. The Wampanoag people called him *pinese*, a title given to only a few of the bravest and wisest warriors.

At Plymouth there soon was a warm friendship between Hobomok and Captain Miles Standish. The other Pilgrims also admired and respected the handsome, dignified pinese. When the land at Plymouth was divided into lots, the Pilgrims gave one lot to Hobomok and his wife. In time, Hobomok became a Christian. Massasoit did not like this because he felt that the Wampanoag should keep their own religion. Yet he still looked on Hobomok as his best friend. Because of his ties both with the Wampanoag and with the Pilgrims, Hobomok was able to bring the two peoples closer together.

One person did not welcome Hobomok to Plymouth. Squanto was secretly jealous of both Massasoit and Hobomok. He was happy living with the Pilgrims and being their special helper. He wanted to be the Pilgrims' only friend among the Indians.

At the end of that summer of 1621, the Pilgrims found that their acres of corn, planted on the fields of the Patuxet Indians, would yield a rich harvest. For the first time since they had come to America, they had plenty to eat! They decided to hold a feast of thanksgiving and to invite Massasoit and his people to share it with them.

Squanto carried the invitation to the sachem at Sowams.

7. Thanksgiving Day

The idea of a thanksgiving feast was not new to the Indians. Massasoit's people had already held one of their own to thank the Great Spirit for their good harvest. Now the sachem said, "We will go to Patuxet to help our English brothers give thanks in the white men's way."

On a crisp October day he set out for Plymouth with about 90 of his people. They did not go empty-handed to the feast. Some braves carried deer, each fat carcass slung on a pole between two men. Others took wild turkeys and other game.

William Bradford was the new governor at Plymouth. He welcomed Massasoit by having a salute fired from the big cannon. The Indians feared both the noise and fire made by this huge firestick, but not one among the Wampanoag allowed his fear to show.

"It is good to be with English friends again," Massasoit said calmly.

It was a joyful gathering at Plymouth that day. The Wampanoag women shyly watched the Pilgrim women as they hurried between fireplaces and fire pits. Pilgrim girls admired the cornhusk and carved wooden dolls of the Indians, while Wampanoag girls fingered the colorful rag dolls of the Pilgrims. Indian boys and Pilgrim boys played games of tag and ball. They made boats out of wood chips and sailed them in the brook.

Massasoit, Hobomok, and the new governor watched the young men in their friendly wrestling matches and footraces. The Pilgrims taught the Indians an English game of batting a ball through rounded wires stuck into the ground. There was much shouting, rushing about, and wild swinging of bats during the noisy fun.

By the time the company was called to dinner,

The first Thanksgiving

everyone had worked up a good appetite in the brisk salt air. Board and trestle tables had been set up under the sunny sky, and the women spread a delicious feast before their hungry guests.

There were baked lobsters and kettles of clam chowder, spit-roasted turkeys, and fat geese. Venison had been roasted in the fire pits. The soldiers cut off juicy slices of meat with their swords. Platters piled high with hot bread were passed back and forth the length of the tables. Massasoit and his people especially enjoyed the butter and ate a good deal of it.

When the celebration was over, Massasoit and Governor Bradford promised each other that they would repeat the feast the following year, and every year thereafter.

8. Trouble with Plymouth

About this time Massasoit was faced with a new problem. Hobomok came to Sowams one day with a warning for the sachem. Squanto was plotting with the Massachusetts Indians to make trouble between Massasoit and the people of Plymouth. The Narragansett, Hobomok said, might also be in the plot.

Massasoit was a good-natured, mild-tempered chief. At first he was unwilling to believe that

Squanto would want to harm him. Then he learned that Squanto had told the Pilgrims that he, Massasoit, was coming with the Narragansett to attack Plymouth.

"Squanto has gone too far!" he cried angrily.

He handed his great knife to a trusted messenger. "Take this knife to the governor at Plymouth!" he told the messenger. "He has seen it and will know that it comes from me. Tell him that Squanto is a traitor to his sachem. The governor must send him to me so that I can punish him with death."

The governor of Plymouth and his council were alarmed and worried by Massasoit's demand. Hobomok had told them of Squanto's plot. They knew that Massasoit was within his rights in asking that Squanto be sent to him for punishment. Yet all of them loved Squanto in spite of all the trouble he was causing. How could they send him to Sowams to be killed?

"What can we do?" the governor asked his councilmen. "Massasoit has been a good friend. The Narragansett would have come to fight us before now, if Massasoit had not stood firmly on our side. But now he asks for the life of our other friend, Squanto."

"We have no choice," one man replied. "Squanto is Massasoit's man, as we are the men of King

James. If we do not hand him over, the sachem may come to take him."

"At least we can beg Massasoit to have pitty on Squanto," another Pilgrim said.

Squanto was brought to the council house. "Don't let Massasoit's messenger take me!" he pleaded.

At that moment one of the councilmen happened to look out of the window. He saw a strange ship outside Plymouth harbor. When he pointed the ship out to the others, the governor and councilmen became very excited. The ship could belong to some country that was at war with England! The governor saw this new problem as an excuse to put off making a decision about Squanto.

"I must see what ship that is," he told Massasoit's messenger.

He and the other Pilgrims stepped quickly from the council house. Squanto followed. He dared not remain alone with the messenger.

The angry messenger returned alone to Sowams. "The English refuse to give Squanto up," he told the sachem.

Massasoit became very angry. The Pilgrims had broken their treaty! Yet, because he had promised to be their friend, he did not want to make war on them. There were other ways of showing his anger!

Word went out from the sachem to all the Wampanoag hunters. They must stop trading their furs at Plymouth! The Pilgrims were very much troubled because Massasoit stopped the fur trade. They needed the money they made on the furs in order to buy supplies from England! They were troubled also because they knew that they had broken faith with Massasoit.

Those were unhappy days at Plymouth. Weeks passed, and Massasoit continued to "frown," as the Pilgrims put it. Only the fact that Hobomok was still living at Plymouth gave hope that the Pilgrims' friendship with Massasoit might be saved.

One day a swift-footed messenger brought sad news to Hobomok.

"Our great sachem is ill unto death. All the magic and medicines of the medicine men have failed to cure him."

Hobomok's heart grew heavy with grief. "I will go to Massasoit at once," he said.

Edward Winslow asked if he might go along with Hobomok. "I will take some English medicine to Massasoit," he said.

The pinese and the Englishman traveled to Sowams at a swift pace.

"My beloved sachem! Better that I should die than he!" Hobomok moaned as they hurried along the trail.

Winslow tried to comfort him. "My medicine may cure him."

"Oh, pray that we be in time, Winslow! He must not die! The world has never seen another like my great sachem. Kind and loving is he to his friends. And reasonable, even to those who have hurt him."

When they arrived at Sowams, they found the people of the village greatly upset. Weeping, wailing Indians were crowding all around the sachem's wigwam. Inside, Massasoit lay with his eyes closed and his face burning with fever. His children had been taken to the wigwam of a relative. The saunk was weeping as she rubbed his arms and legs. A number of medicine men were dancing around them, howling, and shaking rattles.

The medicine men were trying to scare away the evil spirits that had made Massasoit sick. Hobomok asked them to leave the wigwam. "Your spells have failed," he said. "Now with the help of the Great Spirit, we will try this Englishman's new medicine."

Winslow forced medicine between Massasoit's teeth. By the next day the fever was gone. Massasoit opened his eyes and recognized Hobomok and Winslow. He whispered weakly that he was glad to see them. "Winslow came to help you," Hobomok said.

"Massasoit will never forget that you saved his life," the grateful sachem told Winslow.

He thanked Winslow by stopping his quarrel with the Plymouth settlers. He even allowed the Pilgrims to set up a trading post at Sowams. There the Wampanoag hunters traded their rich furs of beaver, otter, and ermine for the small mirrors, metal fishhooks, and knives of the English.

9. A Dream of Friendship Fades

Edward Winslow and the other early writers of New England told of the happy family life of the Indians. Massasoit and the saunk were loving, careful parents. The sachem's big wigwam was a place where all the members of the family were glad to help one another. There were jokes and laughter. The children had a good time, but they also were taught to respect the religion and traditions of the tribe.

The sachem was proud of his handsome children. He had a daughter, Mionie, and three sons named Wamsutta, Metacom, and Sunconewhew.

At the invitation of Governor Bradford and his council, Massasoit took Wamsutta and Metacom on a visit to Plymouth. They were dressed in their finest doeskins with fringe at every seam. The saunk had beautifully embroidered their tunics and

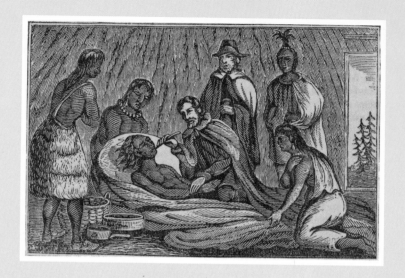

Edward Winslow saves Massasoit's life with the
white man's medicine.

moccasins with shells and quills. Their headbands
and belts were of royal purple shells called Wam-
pum. The tall sachem and his sons made a grand
picture as they strode along Plymouth Street. The
Pilgrims welcomed them as they would have welcomed any visiting king and princes.

The Pilgrim leaders gave the two young
Wampanoag names from the ancient history of
the white man's world. To Wamsutta, who would
one day succeed his father as sachem, they gave
the name of Alexander. Metacom's English name
was Philip. From that time on they were known

by these names among the settlers. Yet at home in Wampanoag country, Massasoit's sons always used their Indian names. This pleased their father because he liked the sound of the Wampanoag names.

"Perhaps someday our Wampanoag names will be all that is left to us," he told his children sadly. "Sometimes it seems as if the English will never be satisfied until they have *all* our land."

With a friendly spirit Massasoit had always listened to the English when they asked for more land. He did not realize the great value of the vast areas that he was giving away. Nor did he know that the price of the kettles, mirrors, and other trade goods that the Pilgrims gave the Indians in return was very little indeed. It pleased him to see the saunk and Mionie wearing dresses of red English cloth. He also liked to have his food cooked in an iron kettle. Yet now, everywhere he looked, he saw that English settlers were closing in on the Wampanoag hunting grounds. Soon the Indians would have no place to hunt and fish!

He was sad to think that he might have hurt his people by giving so much land to his English friends.

Perhaps this doubt of his own wisdom was the reason that Massasoit now began to call himself by his boyhood name of Ousamequin. He might have thought that he was no longer worthy of being called the Great One.

Yet to his people he would always be Massasoit, the head chief of all New England.

As the years passed, more and more English settlers came across the Atlantic Ocean to New England. The greed and hostility of these people hurt and angered Massasoit.

The high-handed way the settlers had of taking over Indian land awoke the fury of many lesser chiefs. "Gather your war parties, great sachem, and sweep these strangers off our tribal lands!" they urged Massasoit.

Wamsutta and Metacom agreed with the chiefs, but Massasoit did not want to make war.

"I have made a treaty of peace," he declared firmly. "I will stand by it, even though the English forget that they, too, have pledged themselves to friendship and justice for both sides."

"But the English no longer act like friends," Metacom said angrily. "See how they try to force us to live like Englishmen and to worship the Great Spirit as they do! They will leave us nothing of our own."

"We will keep our good ways as Indians," Massasoit promised his children, "and worship the Great Spirit as our forefathers did before us."

The settlers were determined that the Indians

should give up their old way of life. The old sachem's ways made them angry. Yet, in spite of their anger and impatience, the people of Plymouth still respected Massasoit. While he lived they dared not push his people as hard as they wished to do.

Massasoit died in 1661, mourned not only by his own people, but by the Pilgrims he had befriended. The people of Sowams pulled down his wigwam. Now his spirit would be free to journey to the Happy Land in the Southwest, where Kiehtan the Great Spirit awaited him. Never again, except at the time of some grand ceremony, when the roll of the greatest chiefs was called, would the Wampanoag speak the name of Massasoit.

After Massasoit's death, the Indians and the English settlers became more and more unfriendly toward each other. Within a few years open war broke out between them. No echo of war whoops and musket shots, nor smell of burning settlements, upset Massasoit's rest beneath the pines near Sowams. He had always kept the dream of friendship with the Pilgrims fresh in his heart. With honor he had kept the treaty he had made on his first visit to the weak little settlement at Patuxet.

About Massasoit's People

The Wampanoags were a group of Algonquian Indians
who lived in the woodlands of Massachusetts and Rhode
Island. These peaceful Indians lived in dome-shaped wigwams covered with birchbark and reeds woven into mats.
They hunted, fished, and gathered nuts and berries for
food. Games of skill and competition were popular. The
Wampanoags worshiped nature and believed their dreams
were sent by their gods to guide and help them. The map
below shows Plymouth, the town which the Pilgrims built
on the site of an old Indian village, and Sowams, where
Massasoit lived.

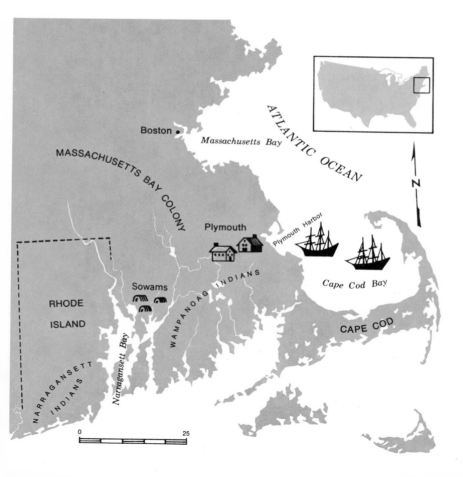

Tecumseh

Shawnee Warrior-Statesman

by James McCague

Where are the Pequot? Where are the Narragansett, the Mohican, the Pocanet, and other powerful tribes of our people? They have vanished
before the avarice and oppression of the white
man, as snow before the summer sun. . . . Will
we let ourselves be destroyed in our turn, without making an effort worthy of our race?

Tecumseh

49

1. A Day of Sorrow

Tecumseh sat up in bed and rubbed his eyes. It was a chilly October morning in 1774.

The young Indian boy had been dreaming that the Long Knives were chasing him. They were strange, pale-faced men with swords like large hunting knives, who came from a land far to the east. He was glad it was only a dream.

Then all of a sudden he shivered. The dream could come true!

Years before, the Long Knives had made a treaty with Tecumseh's people, the Shawnees. They had promised to stay away from the Indian lands north of the great Ohio River. Recently, however, they had broken their promise and started to settle in Shawnee country.

Just a few days ago, the Shawnees had heard that an army of Long Knives was on the march to attack them. Tecumseh's father, chief of one of the five Shawnee clans, and his older brother, Chiksika, had gone off to fight that army. All the warriors in their village had gone too. Since then, there had been no news.

All at once Tecumseh heard dogs barking and people running about outside his bark-covered wigwam. Beside him his little brother, Lowalusika, woke up. Lowalusika was only three years old. He was frightened and began to cry.

Throwing back the buffalo robe that covered their bed, Tecumseh ran outside. The boys lived in a village on the banks of the Scioto River, in the land now called Ohio. In those long-ago times, all of Ohio belonged to the Shawnees and other Indian tribes.

A big crowd had gathered in the center of the village around a group of warriors. As Tecumseh ran to join them, an old man hobbled past. "*Hou!*" he shouted. "It's all over."

Tecumseh's heart sank. He saw his older sister, Tecumapase, trying to give comfort to their mother, Methotasa. The tears streamed down Methotasa's face. Tecumseh's beloved seventeen-year-old brother, Chiksika, was there too.

Chiksika was tall and strong and already a warrior. Under the stripes of red, yellow, and blue warpaint, his face was sad. He came and put his hand on Tecumseh's shoulder.

"I have bad news, little brother. Our father, Chief Pucksinwah, is dead."

Tecumseh felt numb inside. He couldn't answer.

"There was a great battle by the Ohio River,"

said Chiksika. "We fought bravely and killed many Long Knives, but a bullet pierced Pucksinwah's heart. We fought on for a while without him, but then more of the Long Knives came. There were too many of them. We had to run away."

Tecumseh shut his eyes tightly. He was a chief's son; no one must see him cry. "What will happen now?" he asked.

Chiksika shook his head. "The great chief of all the Shawnees has called a council to decide whether we should fight on. Many of our people think that the Long Knives are too strong. They say we must give up now."

"Never!" shouted Tecumseh. He lifted his chin high. "I will go and fight the Long Knives myself and kill them all!"

His big brother smiled gently. "Those are big words for such a small warrior," he said. "Be patient, little brother. Your time will come."

2. Growing-up Years

"Our people have made peace with the Long Knives," Chiksika said to Tecumseh one day later that autumn. It was a good peace. The white men agreed to keep their old promise and stay south of the Ohio River. Thus, all the land north of the river was left to the Indians.

As time went by, however, the white men broke their word once more. White families crossed the Ohio River and built cabins. They shot Indians who went near them. In return, Shawnee warriors started to raid the white settlements.

Tecumseh still longed to be able to join the warriors. For the moment, though, he was busy learning to fish, to trap small animals, and to paddle a canoe. He wrestled and played games with other boys his age.

When Tecumseh was twelve years old, he made a new friend, Sinninatha. He was a white boy who had been captured and adopted into the Shawnee tribe. Sinninatha seemed content to be a Shawnee. He was always so cheerful and pleasant that Tecumseh couldn't help liking him.

One evening as they sat by the village campfire, Tecumseh asked, "Did you have a Long-Knife name, Sinninatha?"

The other boy nodded. "Yes, I did. I was called Stephen Ruddell."

"It sounds funny," Tecumseh laughed. Then he began to point at various things nearby. "*Acohqua*," he said. "*Il-le-nah-lui. Weshe.* What are those in Long-Knife talk?"

Sinninatha had to think hard, for it had been a long time since he had spoken English. At last he named each thing. "Kettle. Arrow. Dog."

A strange excitement took hold of Tecumseh. "You must teach me this talk," he cried.

"Well, all right. But why?"

"I don't know, but you must," Tecumseh said. To himself he thought, "The Long Knives are my enemies, and it is good to know all we can about our enemies."

Sinninatha jumped up and ran to his hut. He came back with a small, leather-covered object. "This is a book—an English Bible," he explained. "Some warriors took it from a cabin they burned not long ago, but they don't know what it's for. Do you?"

"Book?" Tecumseh frowned. "Bi-bel?"

Sinninatha opened the book. "See these marks. They stand for words, as if the person who made the marks is speaking to you. In this way the words are never forgotten."

Tecumseh clapped·a hand over his mouth in amazement. He turned the book's pages. "Long Knives must be very wise," he said thoughtfully. "There is great power in such a thing. I will learn these marks also."

And so he did. He studied until he could speak English almost as well as Sinninatha. Reading and writing were harder, but Tecumseh practiced every day and in time he became fairly good at both.

These were busy years for Tecumseh. Chiksika

was training him to use bow and arrow, tomahawk and war club. He taught the boy to ride a
horse and to hunt deer, bear, and buffalo. From
his big brother, too, Tecumseh learned the meaning of honor.

"Only weak people can lie or cheat," Chiksika
told his brother. "Remember that always."

Sometimes Lowalusika joined in the lessons. The
youngest brother was growing into a scrawny, ugly
little boy. Even worse, he was lazy. "I won't
work! I'll use my wits," he boasted. "Who wants
to be a warrior, anyway?"

Tecumseh was fond of his little brother, but
such talk made him angry. Chiksika calmed
Tecumseh. "Let him alone," he would say.
"Each of you must decide for himself what
kind of man he will be."

3. The Long Knives

Chiksika sent for Tecumseh one day. "You have
seen fifteen summers and fifteen winters," he said.
"You are old enough now to put on warpaint.
Will you come with us to raid the Long Knives?"

Tecumseh's heart pounded. He had worked hard
to become a warrior. "Now I will prove myself,"
he thought as he ran to get his weapons.

With Chiksika in the lead, the small band of

Shawnees rode south to the Ohio River. White settlers coming to Indian country often floated downriver in flatboats. The war party decided to attack the first boat that came along.

They were in luck. A scout soon brought word that a flatboat had landed some distance upstream. Tecumseh crept silently along the riverbank with the other warriors. Then he saw the Long Knives through the bushes. They were cooking their supper over a campfire.

Tecumseh counted thirteen men. They all had guns. He felt chills run up and down his back. "Be strong!" he told himself fiercely. "Be brave!"

Chiksika aimed his long rifle. *Bang!* A white man sprawled on the ground. Instantly, every warrior yelled out the shrill Shawnee war cry. Other rifles cracked. Tecumseh pulled his bow-string. His arrow flew straight and true. Down went a white man who had been standing by the fire.

Tecumseh ran toward the enemy. A bullet whistled past his ear. A big Long Knife swung his rifle at him like a club. Another warrior struck the Long Knife. Carefully, he aimed his tomahawk. . . .

Suddenly it was all over. White men were strewn on the ground. Some Shawnees were wounded, but not one had been killed.

White settlers floating downriver in flatboats
were often attacked by Indians.

"You did well, brother!" Chiksika cried. "How
does it feel to be a warrior?"

To tell the truth, Tecumseh felt dazed. The fight
had been like a wild dream. But his heart nearly
burst with pride at Chiksika's praise.

"*Hou!*" called one of the warriors. "Here's one
that's still alive." He stood over the white man
who was trying feebly to crawl away.

Several warriors seized the wounded man. They
dragged him to a tree and bound him fast with
rawhide thongs. Other warriors piled dry branches
by the tree. One brought a flaming torch.

All at once Tecumseh felt sick. He glanced at his

brother. Chiksika looked troubled too, but he did nothing to stop the warriors.

"He is our enemy," Tecumseh told himself. "He *should* suffer." Somehow, though, Tecumseh could not believe this. The warriors seemed like wild beasts now, not friends he was fond of. They laughed, mocking the frightened man. Tecumseh could watch no longer.

As he turned away he felt Chiksika touch him. "I, too, am ashamed of this," Chiksika whispered.

"It is so cowardly," cried Tecumseh angrily.

Something inside told him that cruelty was a sign of weakness, not strength. "Surely it is right for us to fight for our homeland," he thought, "but this cannot be the way."

"I am only a young warrior now," he told his brother. "But someday I will be a chief. Then I will put a stop to things like this. I swear it!"

4. A Warrior's End

During the next four years Tecumseh grew tall and strong. He went on many raids with Chiksika. More and more, other Shawnees came to admire them both. "They are two of our best warriors," the people said.

The younger brother, Lowalusika, was growing up too. He was still lazy, but his quick wit often amazed his elders. "That one will be a great medicine man someday," they said. Such talk made Tecumseh proud.

Then came tragedy.

Chiksika and Tecumseh went on a hunting trip south of the Ohio River. The land there, called Kentucky, was an ancient Indian hunting ground. The brothers roamed far to the south and west. Never before had Tecumseh realized what a vast land he lived in. Everywhere, however, he saw the cabins of white settlers.

"Is there no end to them?" Tecumseh wondered. "They are like swarms of grasshoppers covering the land."

The Cherokee Indians who lived in that southern country were fighting the settlers. "We should go to help them," declared Chiksika. "These Cherokees are our friends."

Tecumseh nodded. "Yes, the Long Knives always help each other in battle and so must we."

The brothers joined a Cherokee war party in an attack on one of the settlers' forts. The fort was small and its log fence, or stockade, was not very strong. It stood in a field at the edge of a forest. Firing from the shelter of the trees, the Indians shot down many white men.

At last the Cherokee chief commanded, "Now! We will charge and climb over the wall."

As they broke into the open, a rifle cracked from the fort. Tecumseh heard a choked cry at his side. Turning, he saw Chiksika fall. He knelt at his brother's side, but it was too late. Chiksika was dead. Fury blazed up in the young warrior.

"Come on!" he shouted to the others as he sprang to his feet. "Don't stop! Attack! Attack!"

But the Cherokees held back. "You are cowards!" Tecumseh raged. "Chiksika has met a warrior's end. Are you afraid to die too?"

It was no use. The other warriors had lost heart. Sadly, then, Tecumseh lifted his brother's body in his arms and carried it into the forest.

"I will never forget you, Chiksika," he whispered. "And I will never stop hating the white men. Never!"

5. Bad Times

Soon after Tecumseh returned to his home, scouts brought bad news. A great army of white soldiers was marching into Ohio country.

The word ran like wildfire through all the Shawnee towns. Warriors came riding from other tribes nearby—the Delawares, the Wyandots, the Miamis. "Meet with our chiefs in a council," they said. "The Long Knives threaten us too. We will help you to beat them once and for all."

Tecumseh felt a fierce joy. "Now I will avenge my father Pucksinwah and my brother Chiksika," he thought. He could hardly wait, as he sat in the big Shawnee council hut and listened to the chiefs make their plans.

Blue Jacket, chief of one of the Shawnee clans and a great war leader, stood up. "We will need a wise, brave warrior to lead our scouts," he said. "I choose Tecumseh."

"*Hou!*" cried all the other chiefs. "We know Tecumseh. He is a good choice."

Quietly, yet proudly, Tecumseh rose to his feet. "I will do my best," he said simply.

Thus, in the year 1791, the war began. At first it went well for the Indians. Tecumseh's scouts followed every move the white army made. Then, one cold winter dawn, the Indian warriors attacked. Caught by surprise, the white soldiers fought badly. Many were killed or captured. Others ran for their lives.

Now Tecumseh remembered his vow. "We have fought bravely," he said. "Let us not spoil our victory by needless cruelty."

Many Indians would not listen. White prisoners were tortured and killed. "We have won!" the Indians cried. "That is all that matters."

They were wrong. Soon more white soldiers came. The war went on for four long, bloody years. Tecumseh, Blue Jacket, and the other warriors fought on, but now they were outnumbered. They could no longer stop the white soldiers who marched wherever they pleased. Indian towns were burned, and their cornfields were destroyed. Families had to flee as best they could.

About a hundred Shawnee families, Tecumseh and Lowalusika among them, hid deep in the forest. They spent a hard winter there with barely enough to eat. In the spring a messenger came.

"The Long Knives offer us peace," he said. "We must go to their Fort Greenville to sign the treaty. Will you go with us, Tecumseh?"

"No!" Tecumseh answered. "No treaty will save our land from the white men. Their promises are worthless."

Although they were discouraged, his people cheered him. "Tecumseh, you are our leader," they cried.

So it was that Tecumseh became the chief of his clan.

The messenger went away. Several months later Chief Blue Jacket rode into the village.

"The new treaty has been signed," he said. "This land belongs to the white men now. However, they will let us keep the land farther west, called Indiana Territory. They will build forts there and send a white governor. But the land shall be ours forever."

"Do you believe this?" Tecumseh asked angrily.

Now Blue Jacket shrugged his broad shoulders. "If we fight on, Tecumseh, we will lose everything. But this way, maybe most of the Long Knives will be satisfied."

Tecumseh thought of his father, and Chiksika, and other brave men who had died in battle. He bowed his head. "There has been too much sorrow," he thought.

"Very well," he said. "I will take my people westward. But remember—I have signed no treaty. We will see whether or not the white men keep their promise."

6. A Dream Is Born

The Shawnees and their friends, the Delawares, were holding a council. The council pipe was lighted. Each warrior took a puff. A tall young chief stood up in the firelight. It was Tecumseh.

Peace had lasted for three years. Tecumseh was thirty years old now. He had married a Shawnee woman named Mamate, but she had died, leaving him a baby son. The young chief was known among his people as a wise leader, as well as a strong, brave warrior.

Everyone listened to Tecumseh as he spoke: "Brothers, in our hearts we all know the treaty that was signed at Greenville was wrong. Our lands were given to us by the Great Spirit. No white man has the right to take them."

"*Hou!*" murmured the Indians. "It is so!"

"White settlers pour like a flood into our old homeland," Tecumseh went on. "Soon they will claim this land also. Do any of you doubt it?"

No one answered. Tecumseh picked up a twig from the ground and broke it in two. Then he gathered several twigs into a bundle and handed it to a Delaware warrior. "Break that," he commanded.

The warrior tried, but the bundle was too strong.

"You see?" said Tecumseh. "One tribe alone is like one twig. But many tribes together cannot be broken."

Some of the young men nodded. "His words make sense," they told one another.

"A few tribes did band together to fight the Long Knives a few years ago," Tecumseh said. "And it is true that they were beaten." He paused. His voice grew deep and solemn. "But think how it would be if *every* tribe in this land joined in one great Indian nation. There would be many thousands of us. We could drive the Long Knives off and win our old lands back. Nothing could stop us."

"Tecumseh, this is a dream," an old chief objected.

"Yes, a great dream," said Tecumseh proudly. "And we can make it come true." He lifted his arms. "It will take courage and patience, but we can be a proud, free people again. Who will follow me?"

"We will!" shouted several warriors. "Yes! Yes!" cried others.

Still, some were doubtful. But Tecumseh had made them think. In a few days, runners carried his words to more distant Indian towns. Everywhere, the Indians had been downhearted and discouraged. Now, because of Tecumseh, they felt new hope.

7. Tecumseh and the Prophet

Tecumseh's whole life was now devoted to his plan for a great Indian nation. He journeyed through the Indiana Territory and held councils with the Wyandots and Miamis. Farther west, he talked with the Sacs, Foxes, Potawatomies, and the warlike Sioux.

"We will join you," their chiefs said. "Let us fight the Long Knives now!"

Tecumseh's brother began preaching to the Indians at the command of the Great Spirit. He became known as the Prophet.

"No, we must bide our time," Tecumseh warned them. "Before we fight again, we must be strong enough to sweep every white man from this land."

The chiefs agreed to wait. Meanwhile a strange thing happened.

Lowalusika, Tecumseh's brother, had become a Shawnee medicine man. He had grown up into a small, rather ugly man, and few of the people paid much attention to him. Then a change came over Lowalusika.

First he adopted a new name, Tenskatawah, which meant "One-with-Open-Mouth." The Great Spirit told him to do this, he said. From now on, he claimed, he would speak with the Great

Spirit's voice. Perhaps he truly believed this, for Tenskatawah began to preach to the Indians more strongly than he had preached before.

"Never be friendly with white men," he told them. "You must live clean lives. Be strong! Help one another! Above all, have faith in yourselves and in our great new leader, Tecumseh. The Great Spirit commands this through me—his prophet."

The Shawnees listened. Soon people from other tribes came to listen too. They began to call Tenskatawah the "Prophet." Tecumseh was pleased. "Working together, brother, we cannot fail," he told Tenskatawah. "We must not—and we will not!"

Many Indians left their own tribes and came to join Tecumseh and the Prophet. So many came that after a while the two brothers moved to a new town on the banks of the Tippecanoe River in western Indiana. White men called the place Prophet's Town. These men wondered somewhat nervously what went on there. Yet several years passed, and the peace was not broken.

By 1809, as Tecumseh had foreseen, the whites wanted more land. The governor of Indiana Territory, William Henry Harrison, held council with a few chiefs from the Miami, Delaware, and Potawatomie tribes. He offered them whiskey, rolls of red cloth, food, and other presents. In return he asked them to sign a new treaty, giving up part of Indiana.

These chiefs were weak, foolish men. They wanted the presents, so they signed the treaty.

Tecumseh's people were very angry. "Another white man's trick!" they cried. Others who had not believed Tecumseh before hurried to Prophet's Town. "You were right, Tecumseh," they said. "We will join you now."

One day a white man appeared at Prophet's Town with a letter from Governor Harrison. The governor did not want the Indians to band together as they were doing. "If you try to make war again," the letter warned, "you will get nothing but misery and failure."

The white man read this aloud to all the Indians.

"Tell your governor that I will go and talk this over with him," said Tecumseh.

More than 300 warriors went to Vincennes with their chief. White soldiers were lined up to meet them. Governor Harrison stood there—a sturdy, broad-shouldered man in a uniform trimmed with shiny gold braid. He had piercing dark eyes under heavy brows.

Tecumseh looked tall and stately in a fine buckskin shirt and leggings. He wore a red blanket around his shoulders and two eagle feathers in his hair. He and Harrison shook hands. The meeting began in a grove of trees outside the town.

"We come in peace, but we cannot be friends if you keep taking our land," Tecumseh declared.

"My government bought the land," insisted Harrison. "It is ours now."

"The land belongs to all the tribes," Tecumseh argued. "A few chiefs had no right to sell it."

They talked on, but neither man would yield. At last Harrison said coldly, "This meeting is over. I will tell the president of the United States what you have said, Tecumseh. He will decide about the land. I warn you, though—we mean to keep it."

The two men stared at each other. Each knew that he was facing a strong, bold enemy.

The meeting between Tecumseh and Harrison ended in a bitter argument.

8. A Brother's Folly

Tecumseh hurried back to Prophet's Town. There he gathered 20 of his best warriors. "Quickly! We must make ready for a long journey," he commanded. Then he turned toward Tenskatawah.

"We have no time to lose," he said. "Governor Harrison has made it plain that we will have to fight to save this Indiana land. Most of the northern tribes will fight with us. Now I must get the southern tribes to join us too."

The Prophet's eyes gleamed. "Death to the Long Knives!" he cried.

"Patience, brother," said Tecumseh. "There must be no trouble until we are ready. I think Harrison may attack you while I am gone. If he does, take our people and run away. Promise me that, Tenskatawah. I am counting on you."

"I promise," he answered gravely.

Tecumseh and his band rode far south into the land that is now Florida. All along the way the tribes knew of his great fame. They greeted him and his warriors joyfully. He held solemn councils with the Cherokees, the Creeks, the Choctaws, the Chickasaws, and the Seminoles.

"Everywhere I see white settlers," he told them. "They chop down your forests. They kill the wild animals you need for food. Soon they will take your land away altogether, and you will have nowhere to go."

"It is true," said the Indians sadly.

"We must stop them before it is too late," Tecumseh said. "Will you join your northern brothers?" Carefully he explained his plan for a mighty Indian nation.

"We will join," they agreed.

Tecumseh gave a packet of red sticks to every chief. "Each time the moon is full, burn one stick," he said. "When the last stick is burned, the Great Spirit will give you a sign. Then gather your warriors and march north to meet me."

"To fight?" asked some of the chiefs.

"When they see our great strength, the Long Knives may be afraid to fight," said Tecumseh. "Then we can have a fair and lasting peace. But if we must fight—we will!"

Only one chief hung back. This was Big Warrior, of the Creeks. To him, Tecumseh said scornfully, "When I return home I will stamp my foot. The earth will shake. Your village will fall down. Rivers will flow backward and the sun will hide its face. That will be the sign I spoke of."

Big Warrior became very frightened. "Tecumseh, don't be angry," he begged. "I will join you."

Finally Tecumseh rode homeward. He was pleased with his work. As his men crossed the Ohio River, they saw a warrior from Prophet's Town waiting on the north bank.

"Bad news!" the warrior cried. "All is lost!" Quickly he told his story.

"A short time ago, Harrison marched toward our town with many soldiers. Your brother, the Prophet, disobeyed your orders. He urged us to fight. He told us he had magic powers. No white man's bullet could hurt us, he said—"

Tecumseh scowled. "Go on; and then—?"

"We were fools, Tecumseh. We really believed him. We attacked the soldiers, but the Prophet had lied. Their bullets killed many of us. The Prophet himself ran away. We all ran. Then Harrison's men burned Prophet's Town."

A hot, blind rage filled Tecumseh, but he controlled himself, with an effort.

"We have been betrayed," Tecumseh's warriors shouted furiously. "The Prophet must die!"

"No, let him live with his shame," Tecumseh said. "That will be a worse punishment. Forget him. We must try to undo this harm he has done." But Tecumseh's heart was heavy. Would his followers stand by him now, or would they be afraid?

He did not know.

9. When the Earth Shook

From a new camp far in the woods, Tecumseh sent trusted messengers to the other tribes. Soon he knew the worst. Most of those tribes had lost their faith just as he had feared. They would follow him no longer.

Then a British officer in a red coat made his way to Tecumseh's camp. He came from Canada.

"My country, England, plans to make war on the Americans," he told Tecumseh. "America once belonged to us. Then the Long Knives fought us and won their freedom."

"I know," Tecumseh nodded.

"Now we are going to win back this land," said the Englishman. "If you help us, we will give all your old homeland back to you. Our king promises this."

Tecumseh talked with his few loyal warriors. "I don't trust *any* white man," he declared. "Still, these redcoats need our help. Therefore, they may keep their promise. I think we must take the chance. What do you say?"

"We say yes!" the warriors cried.

Later, that autumn of 1811, an earthquake shook the land. Trees and houses tumbled down. The Ohio River flowed backward. Clouds of dust boiled up and hid the sun. It was the sign

Tecumseh had described to Big Warrior, but it came too late.

The southern tribes had heard of Governor Harrison's victory over the Prophet. They were afraid to join Tecumseh now. Even the tribes nearby decided to wait.

The following June, England and the United States went to war. At once, Tecumseh led 70 warriors to Fort Malden, in Canada. "We have come to fight," he told General Isaac Brock, the British leader.

General Brock was a kind and honorable man who liked the Indians. He was a forceful, courageous leader, but he had only a few soldiers. Across the river which formed the boundary between the United States and Canada stood the town of Detroit. Many American soldiers were on duty there.

"They are too strong for us to attack," said Brock.

"No! Strike now!" Tecumseh urged. "We can capture Detroit." He took out his knife. On a piece of birchbark he scratched a map showing the best way to attack. The general was impressed.

"Very well," he said.

With his warriors and a few redcoats, Tecumseh crossed the river. The Indians hid in the woods around Detroit, cutting off all approaches by land.

Now the town could not get help or supplies. Brock then crossed the river with his men and prepared to attack. Tecumseh joined him.

Then Tecumseh ordered his Indians out of the woods. Whooping wildly, they circled round and round the town. The American general was terrified. He thought Tecumseh had many more men than he did. So the general surrendered Detroit without a fight.

"No prisoner will be harmed," Tecumseh promised the Americans. "We show our manhood in battle, not by killing helpless people."

General Brock was so pleased with Tecumseh that he gave him a sword and a fine red coat. He took the silken sash from his own waist and tied it around Tecumseh's.

"Now you are a British general," he said.

Tecumseh smiled. He took the sash and gave it to another chief named Roundhead. "This honor belongs to all of us," he said. "Brother warriors, we have made a good beginning."

10. The Siege of Fort Meigs

Riding a big black horse, Tecumseh led more than 700 warriors out of Detroit. News of the great victory had brought Indian warriors hurrying to his side, eager to fight.

"We will never doubt you again, Tecumseh," they said.

British soldiers marched beside the Indians. The sun gleamed on warpaint and red coats. Muskets and tomahawks glittered. Big iron cannons rolled along, pulled by straining oxen. The army was on its way to attack the Americans' Fort Meigs in northern Ohio.

Another British general, Henry Proctor, had taken General Brock's place. He was fat and haughty, and Tecumseh didn't like him. Still, the army was so strong that victory seemed certain. Tecumseh's heart beat fast with pride and hope.

Fort Meigs was a strong place, built of stones and thick logs. William Henry Harrison, Tecumseh's old enemy, was in command there. Cannon muzzles stuck out of the walls on every side.

"My cannons are bigger," General Proctor boasted. "We will knock this fort to pieces."

The British gunners fired. Again and again the cannons thundered. Through clouds of smoke, Tecumseh and his warriors attacked, but the Americans had held their fire. Now bullets and cannonballs flew from the walls. The Indians were driven back.

For two weeks the fighting went on.

Then more American soldiers marched up from the south. They fell on the British and Indians by surprise. But suddenly Tecumseh saw his chance. "Pretend to run away!" he cried.

The Indians ran, with the yelling soldiers in pursuit. The land was covered with dense woods and thickets. Soon the Americans were strung out in disorder. "Now!" Tecumseh shouted. "Turn and fight!"

The warriors, who had stayed together as they fled, turned and pounced on their enemies like wildcats. Rifle balls and tomahawks cut the Americans down. Some ran pell-mell back to Fort Meigs, but many threw down their guns and surrendered.

As they led their prisoners back to camp, the warriors were still filled with the madness of battle. Some of them began to kill the Americans. Tecumseh galloped up from the battlefield just in time. Leaping from his horse, he seized two warriors and flung them to the ground. He whipped out his war club.

"Who dares to defy Tecumseh?" he roared.

The warriors shrank away in fear. Immediately the chief's terrible anger left him. "Have you forgotten my teachings so easily?" he cried. "Oh, my poor brothers, what will become of you?"

General Proctor had watched all this and he

Tecumseh rushes in to prevent his braves from murdering captured white soldiers.

had done nothing. "Why didn't *you* protect these prisoners?" Tecumseh asked.

"Sir," answered General Proctor stiffly, "your Indians cannot be commanded." Actually, he had been afraid.

"Go away!" Tecumseh thundered. "You are unfit to command. Go and put on petticoats!" He turned away in despair. Proctor was a weak man, he knew now.

For the first time, Tecumseh felt doubt. How could the British win a war with such a leader?

11. The Last Battle

General Proctor ordered his army to retreat.

"Do you expect to win by running away?" Tecumseh asked in disgust.

But the general would not listen. He marched the army all the way back to Detroit. Scouts brought word that William Henry Harrison was following with a strong American force. Still Proctor would not fight. He gave up Detroit and led his men across the river to Fort Malden.

"I was wrong to trust the British," Tecumseh told his warriors bitterly. "They lie to us, like all white men. If you want to leave me now, I won't blame you."

"No, Tecumseh, we will stay," the warriors said.

More bad news came. British and American warships had fought a battle on Lake Erie. The Americans had won. At that, General Proctor left Fort Malden and retreated again. But now Harrison's army was close behind.

Tecumseh went to Proctor's tent. He stood there, tall and stern in his red coat. "You are like a dog that puts its tail between its legs and runs away," he said. "Go! My people and I will fight alone."

Stung by Tecumseh's scorn, General Proctor ordered his army to stop retreating. They were camped on high ground several miles north of Lake Erie. On one side ran a river called the Thames. On the other was a swamp. It was a good place to make a stand. But Tecumseh had lost hope now. He called his warriors together.

"Brothers, tomorrow we go into battle," he told them. "I will fall in that battle."

He unbuckled his British sword and handed it to a warrior. "Give this to my son when he grows to manhood," he said. He took off his red coat and put on a buckskin shirt. Watching, the Indians felt their blood run cold. Somehow they knew that Tecumseh spoke the truth.

The next morning the British and Indians lined up for battle. Across the field they saw their enemies coming. With a crash of rifles, the Americans charged. The British line broke, and

General Proctor wheeled his horse and galloped off. British soldiers began to surrender.

Now a great mass of Americans on horseback came dashing toward the Indians' line. "Hold your fire till they draw near," Tecumseh shouted.

The rifles spat flame. Many of the Americans tumbled from their saddles, but the rest came on. The fighting raged back and forth. Tecumseh ran at a tall American officer, lifting his war club for a mighty blow. The American raised a pistol and fired.

There was a flash, a roar. Tecumseh fell.

The death of Tecumseh at the Battle of the Thames.

"Tecumseh is dead!" At that dread cry, the Indians turned and melted into the surrounding forest. Suddenly the battle was over.

Late that night, says an old Indian legend, some Shawnee warriors stole back to the battlefield. Silently and sadly they bore Tecumseh's body to a spreading tree beside the Thames River. There, in a secret grave, they buried their great chief.

Tecumseh's dream of a proud, free Indian nation had ended forever.

Years of peace followed. The Indians lived as best they could in the white men's America which grew and prospered. As time passed, even the white men came to admire Tecumseh for his bravery and his high ideals. In a strange sort of way, their own nation was much like the one he had tried to build.

About Tecumseh's People

The Shawnees were Algonquian Indians living in the Ohio
River country. They lived in large villages of roomy wigwams, which could be taken down and moved easily when
necessary. The Shawnees grew corn, hunted, and once a
year traveled to the western plains to hunt buffalo. The
map below shows Kispoko Town, where Tecumseh lived
as a boy; Prophet's Town, where the Indians were defeated in the Battle of Tippecanoe; and the Thames River,
north of Lake Erie, where Tecumseh was killed in battle.

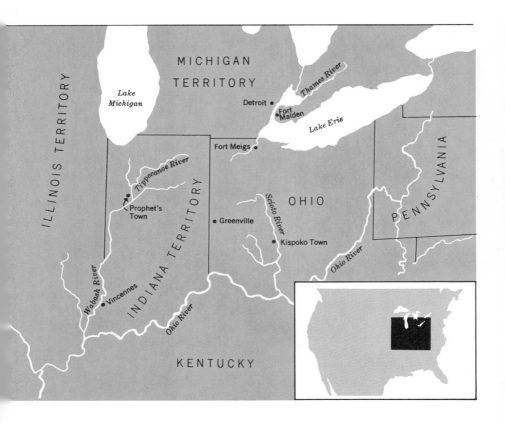

Black Hawk

Indian Patriot

by LaVere Anderson

The rapids of Rock River furnished us with an
abundance of excellent fish, and the land, being
good, never failed to produce good crops. . . .
Here our village had stood for more than a hundred years. . . . But, how different is our situation
now. . . . Then we were as happy as the buffalo
on the plains—but now, we are as miserable as
the hungry, howling wolf in the prairie!

Black Hawk

1. Brave Sauk Boy

"Rock River is dangerous today," Black Hawk told himself.

He stood on the shore and looked across the brown water. Heavy spring rains had made the river flood so that it spread far beyond its banks. Along the shore the water covered bushes and hid the lower branches of trees. The Sauk Indian boy had never seen the river run so high and swift as now.

"I'm glad I'm not out there in a canoe," he thought.

On this spring morning in 1777, Black Hawk and his father were out hunting. His father's name was Pyesa. He was a war chief of the Sauk Indians, who lived in what is now western Illinois.

Pyesa had gone up on a high bluff, following the tracks of a deer. Black Hawk was hunting small game along the river. Suddenly he saw an opossum. It sat in a tree far from dry land. Flood water rose high up the trunk of the tree.

The boy smiled. He knew opossums did not like water. The furry little animal meant to sit in that tree until the river went down.

"I have other plans for you," Black Hawk said softly. "My mother will welcome you for her cooking pot."

He fitted an arrow to his small bow. Then he stopped and shook his head. If he shot the opossum, it would fall into the water and wash downstream in the swift current.

"I will go out there and catch it with my hands," he decided.

He laid his bow and arrows on dry ground and kicked off his moccasins. When he stepped into the river, the cold, muddy water came to his ankles. Two more steps and it reached his knees. Slowly he moved forward. Now the water was above his waist.

He started to swim, but it was hard work battling the current. He was glad when a few strokes brought him to the tree. He pulled himself up onto a branch. The opossum snarled and showed its sharp teeth from a branch above. "It's no use fighting me," he told the animal. "I have caught many like you."

Suddenly Black Hawk heard a voice shouting, "Help! Help me!" Startled, he turned and saw Francis St. Clair, the French trader, in a canoe upstream. St. Clair came to the Sauk village every spring to trade for the furs that the Indians had trapped. The Sauks liked him.

St. Clair was in trouble. His canoe had been caught in a tangle of bushes and low branches. It twisted and bucked in the racing water. The trader was trying to get free before the canoe overturned.

"Come and help me!" he called to Black Hawk. Then he stood up and pushed hard at a branch with his paddle. The canoe spun around in a circle. St. Clair's head struck another branch. Down he went into the water. The canoe, still upright, became wedged among the bushes.

Black Hawk gasped. He knew St. Clair must be hurt. "He'll drown!" thought the boy in horror.

He watched from the tree as the water carried the trader downstream toward him. One slender branch of Black Hawk's tree stretched low over the flood water.

"If I can crawl out there, perhaps I can grab him before the river carries him past," Black Hawk thought.

As he carefully crept along the branch, he felt it sway under his weight. Beneath him the river raged and boiled around floating logs and jagged tree limbs. Black Hawk held his breath. He kept his eyes on St. Clair's head bobbing above the water. Nearer and nearer it came.

Far out on the swaying branch, Black Hawk braced himself and stretched one hand toward the trader. The shaggy brown head was just beyond his fingers.

The boy strained forward another inch, every muscle tense. St. Clair's tangled hair brushed his hand. Quickly Black Hawk wound the hair about his fist and lifted the man's head above water. St. Clair gasped, and his hands made feeble swimming motions.

"Be easy," Black Hawk warned. "I'll get you to shore."

But how? the boy wondered. It was plain that St. Clair could not help himself.

Black Hawk's arm began to ache from the pull of St. Clair's weight. The branch snapped danger- ously. Suddenly he was afraid of the cruel water racing beneath him. His fingers loosened on the trader's hair. Then shame swept over him. He could not let fear stop him from saving his friend. His fingers tightened again on St. Clair's hair.

Black Hawk moved back along the branch. Again it cracked. His arm was shaking now, and he panted for breath as he fought the river for St. Clair's life.

"I'll—get—you—to—shore," he gasped his prom- ise again.

"And I will help you, my son," said a deep voice.

Black Hawk turned in surprise. There in the

water, swimming strongly, was his father. Pyesa put a powerful arm around the trader. "We will swim together," he told St. Clair.

The trader heard him and nodded. *"Wach-e-ton,"* Pyesa said. "Good." Slowly the two men made their way to shore. Black Hawk swung into the water and followed them. The forgotten opossum sat in the tree and watched.

2. Thunder God Speaks

"Father, you came just in time," Black Hawk said as they all rested on shore.

Chief Pyesa smiled. "After I killed the deer, I looked for you. I was on the high bluff when I saw you rescue our friend."

"You have a brave son, Pyesa," St. Clair said. Like most traders of that region, he spoke the Sauk language.

"We will get some dry clothes for you in the village," Pyesa said. "I will send some boys for your canoe."

They started for the Sauk village a short distance away. The Sauks, who were sometimes called Sacs, belonged to the eastern forest tribes of Indians. Black Hawk's village, Saukenuk, lay on a beautiful point of land between the Rock River and the Mississippi River. It was the largest Indian village in this part of the country. Around a center square stood more than 100 lodges covered with elm bark.

In their lodge, Black Hawk's mother, Ketikwe, made hot squirrel stew for St. Clair and gave him dry clothing. Soon the trader felt strong again. Some boys pulled his canoe to shore and brought his trade goods to Black Hawk's lodge. St. Clair spread the goods out for all to see.

There were shining pans and sharp knives, warm blankets and bright-colored cloth. There were beads blue as a summer sky. There was a rifle.

The trader turned to the watching Black Hawk. "Take your choice, my young friend. You saved my life, and I want to thank you with a present."

Black Hawk could scarcely believe his ears, but his eyes went straight to the rifle. A rifle of his own! He could hunt deer with it. In the whole village, no other boy his age had a rifle. He hoped his parents would not think him too young to own so fine a gun.

He looked up at his mother. Ketikwe was gazing at the blue beads. Black Hawk saw a look of longing on her face. If she had those beads, she would sew them onto a handsome deerskin coat for his father. Slowly the boy's eyes went back to the rifle. Then he turned to the trader.

"I will take the blue beads to give to my mother," Black Hawk said.

When he saw the smile of love and happiness on his mother's face, he knew he had made the right choice.

Even without a rifle, Black Hawk was soon hunting deer and learning the other things a young Sauk had to know.

As the months passed, he trapped raccoon, beaver, and muskrat for meat and fur. With his bow and arrows, he shot ducks in the sky and fish in the river. He gathered cattail stalks for mats to carpet his family's lodge. He followed his father on buffalo and deer hunts. He learned the songs and dances of his people and heard the elders tell about great Sauk deeds of the past. At last he was fourteen and ready to go into the deep woods where he would live without food while he waited for his spirit dream.

This was a custom of the Sauks. The Indians believed that a boy's future was foretold by the kind of spirit that came to him in his dream.

In the gray light of a summer morning, Black Hawk awoke early. He hurried to the river and washed himself very clean. Then he went into the woods to a hidden spot he knew. He spread his blanket on the ground and sat upon it cross-legged. All day he sat quietly, without food. A patch of wild turnips grew nearby, but he would not break his fast by eating them.

At night he slept, but he did not have a dream. The second day and night were like the first. He began to worry. Was his future so unimportant that no dream would come to him? He turned his face toward Grandfather Sun.

"Let me dream," he begged the sun spirit.

On the third night he arose from his blanket and began to dance. Higher and higher he leaped, chanting the songs of his people. At last, faint and dizzy, he fell to the ground and slept. He dreamed that a great storm came. Lightning split the sky. Thunder roared. A huge tree burst into flames.

He awoke to find rain beating down on him. As in his dream, lightning flashed and thunder crackled. He rose to his knees. There, on the bluff, was a tree that lightning had set afire. Fear and wonder shook Black Hawk. He had dreamed of the Thunder God, and now the god was speaking! He was the god who gave Sauk men success in war.

"I shall be a great warrior!" Black Hawk thought in awe. "Thunder God came to me in my sleep. He has told me my future."

He rose and picked up his wet blanket. He was so weak that his legs shook under him, but his heart was proud and happy as he started home.

Black Hawk's dream began to come true. When he was fifteen, he went with a war party to raid another Indian tribe and wounded an enemy. That put him in the ranks of the braves. He shaved his head like the other warriors, leaving only a tuft of hair on top. On special occasions he tied a deer tail, dyed red, in his hair.

The Sauks' enemies were the Osages and Sioux. These tribes disliked the strong, warlike Sauks who were quick to fight when others came onto their hunting grounds. The Sauks' close friends were the

In this early print the Sauk and Fox perform a war dance before going to battle.

Fox Indians who lived across Rock River. In time of battle the Sauk and the Fox joined together under one chief.

When Black Hawk was sixteen, he rode beside his father in a war against the Osages who had been hunting on Sauk land. Black Hawk was a handsome young warrior, not tall but strong and quick. He proved his bravery by fearlessly striking an Osage with his tomahawk and killing him.

By the time he was nineteen, Black Hawk was the leader of a band of young warriors. They were bold fighters, for it was through bravery in war that Indian youths proved themselves. Each young man wanted to show his love for his tribe by defending it against enemies. Black Hawk led his courageous band on many successful warpaths.

Then, three years later in another battle over hunting grounds, Chief Pyesa was killed. Sadly his son returned home.

At Saukenuk Black Hawk was called to stand before the elders in the council lodge. The red war paint was still on his face.

Wrinkled old Five Bears said, "Our war chief is dead. You, his son, are young—only 22 winters—but you have shown yourself more skillful in battle and more fearless before danger than any other of our braves. We choose you to be our new war chief."

Black Hawk nodded.

"The Thunder God spoke truly," he thought with pride. "My people have named me a great warrior."

3. A Sad Treaty

Chief Black Hawk sat in the council lodge listening to the angry talk of the tribe's elders.

"Why do the Americans want us to send Redbird to their jail?" demanded one. "We do not want to quarrel with the Americans, but Redbird was not to blame for killing the white man. The white man had been insulting to Redbird's daughter. Besides, Redbird was drunk, and it was the white man who gave him the whiskey."

Black Hawk sighed. It had been fifteen years since he had been chosen as war chief of the Sauk tribe. They had been hard years, for more and more white men were coming onto Sauk land. They had brought whiskey to trade to the Indians. Now a Sauk had killed a trader.

Black Hawk raised a hand to stop the angry talk.

"It is better to do as we are asked," he told the elders. "When Redbird explains what happened, the American Father will set him free."

"American Father" was the Sauks' name for the government of the white men in Washington, D.C.

Redbird was sent to St. Louis, a trading post on the Mississippi River, where the white men had a jail. Time passed, but he did not return. His wife and children blackened their faces with charcoal and fasted in sorrow.

At last Chief Black Hawk declared, "We must send help to Redbird. He may need friends to explain that he is really a good man."

He picked four subchiefs to go to St. Louis to try to help Redbird. Quashquame was to be the spokesman.

On a bright summer morning, the elders gathered to watch the subchiefs leave. The travelers were given four of the best horses and an extra pack horse.

Bright Fox, a young warrior, came running from his lodge. He carried a large bundle.

"Here are the furs," Bright Fox told Quashquame. "I have packed them well."

He laid the big, soft bundle upon the extra horse and tied it firmly with long strings of deerskin. "They are fine furs," Bright Fox said, "muskrat and beaver. The dead trader's family will like them."

The elders heard the young warrior and nodded. "*Wach-e-ton*. Good," they said.

Everybody knew the meaning of the furs. Such a gift was a Sauk custom. It was a payment to the dead man's family known as "covering the blood" that had been spilled. Many families in the village had given their best furs to make the bundle.

Black Hawk stood to one side and watched as the subchiefs mounted their horses. "Ride swiftly," he told them. "Bring Redbird back to his people."

His heart was heavy as he watched the four men ride away. Why must there be so much trouble with the white men? he asked himself. Once the Indians and the white men had been friends. White traders, like the good French trader St. Clair, had been welcome in the village. But now American traders cheated the Indians. They took the Indians' furs and gave rusty pans and broken guns in exchange. Worse still, they sold the Indians whiskey. "Why can we not live as friends again?" Black Hawk thought sadly.

Then his spirits lifted as he saw his wife, Singing Bird, come from their lodge with his children. The oldest boy, Little Eagle, carried a spear. At eight he was already skilled at spearing fish in the river.

"Bring us a good dinner," Black Hawk called.

Little Eagle grinned. *"Hen-e-koh-e,"* he said. "All right."

Slowly the days passed. Late summer berries ripened. In the fields the corn stood high. Horses grew sleek on the rich bluegrass. It was a land of peace and plenty, yet the people were uneasy because no word had come from St. Louis.

With the first sharp winds of fall, it was time for the Sauks to go on their winter hunt. Each year the whole tribe left the village and traveled to their hunting grounds to trap beaver and other small animals. In the spring white men would give the Indians trade goods in exchange for the furs of these animals.

"We will not hunt until the men return with Redbird," Chief Black Hawk said.

Again the people waited. At last the subchiefs returned. They wore fine white man's clothes and had medals on their chests. Redbird was not with them. They met with the chief and elders.

"Where is Redbird?" Black Hawk asked.

"Dead," Quashquame answered. "The white men let him out of jail to see us. Redbird was so happy that he ran to meet us. Then the soldiers shot him. They said he was trying to escape."

He stopped, then said slowly, "That is not all that happened. The American Father will pay the tribe $1,000 a year."

"Why should he do that?" Black Hawk asked in surprise.

Quashquame looked uneasy. "We signed a treaty. It gives the American Father all Sauk land on this side of the Great River and a little of our hunting grounds across the river."

The elders stared. "What right had you to do that?" demanded one. "We did not send you to trade our land. We sent you to bring Redbird home. Only our principal chiefs can sign treaties."

Quashquame replied, "The American Father says he will protect us from other tribes."

"We can protect ourselves!" Black Hawk turned away in anger. His anger grew when he heard

Chief Black Hawk holding the sparrow hawk for which he was named.

Quashquame tell how the white men had given the subchiefs money, clothes, fine food, and much whiskey. The subchiefs had had a good time. Quashquame couldn't remember just when they had signed away millions of acres of Sauk land, including Saukenuk.

"But the American Father says that we can still live here so long as the land is public land," Quashquame hurried to explain. "He will build us a trading post."

The elders talked among themselves. At last one said, "If the American Father promises that we can live here and have a trading post and $1,000 a year, the treaty is not so bad."

Black Hawk smiled bitterly. "I do not trust such promises. The American Father knows that four subchiefs cannot sign away our land. The treaty means nothing."

He was wrong. To the white men, this treaty signed in 1804 meant that the Sauks no longer owned the land of their fathers. It meant that their land in what the Americans called the Northwest Territory had been sold. Someday white men would want to live at Saukenuk. Then the American Father would open the land to settlement by white people, and the Indians would have to move away.

4. White Man's War

"The white men are quarreling among themselves!"

All up and down the Mississippi River, red men smiled as they told one another that news. The American Father was angry because the British Father had stopped American ships on the seas and hurt American trade with other countries. The Americans said the British were stirring up trouble among the Indians too.

One day in 1812, when summer lay softly on the pleasant land, the American Father declared war on the British. At the same time, the government in Washington sent an agent to Saukenuk. The agent said the Indians must not take sides against the Americans. No more British traders from Canada would be allowed on the Mississippi River, but the Sauks could go downriver to trade at Fort Madison. There they would be treated well by the American trader.

Chief Black Hawk listened and rubbed his shaved head. He was thinking that Fort Madison lay far to the south. Where was the trading post for Saukenuk that had been promised? But he said nothing. Let the white men fight if they liked. He had no wish to take sides.

Autumn came. It was time to move to their hunting grounds. The women packed pots and sleeping robes. The men sharpened lances and cleaned guns. Black Hawk took a small party to Fort Madison to get the winter supplies.

At the fort a strange trader greeted them.

"We need ammunition and more guns," Black Hawk said. "We need some strong new traps."

"Where are your trade goods?" asked the white man.

"We will pay you in the spring with the furs we take this winter as we always do," Black Hawk explained.

"Then you must wait until spring for your supplies," came the answer.

"We have always paid the traders in the spring!" Bright Fox spoke up. "How can we hunt with empty guns or take furs without traps?"

The white man shrugged. "From me you get no supplies until you pay."

"Come," Black Hawk told his men. "We will go home."

At Saukenuk a pleasant surprise awaited them. Despite the war, a British trader had come down the Mississippi. He brought guns and ammunition, as well as presents for everybody. The Indians had known and liked him for a long time. They called him the Red Head.

"I bring you a message," he told Black Hawk. "General Dixon wants you to bring 200 of your warriors to Canada and join the British army against the Americans."

"It is not the Sauks' war," Black Hawk said, "and the American Father asked us not to take sides."

"What have the Americans ever done for the Sauks?" demanded the Red Head. "You say their trader would not even trust you for winter supplies. Soon they will drive you from your land. They want it. That is why they had your subchiefs sign the treaty. If you fight with us and we win the war, the British will throw away the treaty. Your land will be yours forever."

Black Hawk's face grew grave. It was true the Americans wanted Sauk land. Lately the white men had been saying it was time for the Sauks to move across the Mississippi to Iowa country. They said it was in the treaty. Black Hawk made up his mind.

"*Hen-e-koh-e*. All right. We will join you," he told the Red Head.

When the trader left, Black Hawk called his elders and warriors together.

"I have never liked the Americans," he said, "but we have had friends among the British. If we fight for the British, we can save our land."

The older men stirred in fear, but the young warriors looked eager. It would be good to go on the warpath against the hated Americans.

Then Keokuk rose to speak. He was partly white and was many years younger than Black Hawk. But he was already a power in the tribe.

"It is not wise to anger the Americans," he said. "They are too strong. If we fight against them, it will lead to trouble."

"We have trouble now," Black Hawk answered. "They say we must leave our homes and move across the Mississippi."

"There are good places across the river," Keokuk said.

Black Hawk stared at him coldly. "It is your

Because Keokuk wanted peace, he moved his band to new homes across the Mississippi. His son and wife are seen below.

white blood that speaks. But I am *all* Indian. I shall join the British and save the land of my fathers."

"I shall stay here," Keokuk replied. "Friendship with the Americans will win more than guns."

Black Hawk soon had 200 braves ready to go with him. They painted their faces with the red paint they kept in clam shells. Their women had packed pemmican for them—food made of dried meat and berries. Every brave hung a small deerskin bag of pemmican from his belt.

The Sauks joined the British army near Detroit, Michigan. Black Hawk was called "General Black Hawk" by the British. That winter the Sauks fought bravely in four battles. They fought in the Indian way, moving silently as shadows, then striking swiftly and slipping away.

"The white men march out into the open and are killed," Bright Fox said with wonder. "Who would take care of our women and children if we let ourselves be killed like that?"

"I do not like the long waits between battles," Horsetail said. "My lance grows dull while we wait."

When summer came again, Black Hawk led his men home. The war was not over, but the young warriors had become restless. They thought the white men's war moved too slowly.

At Saukenuk, Black Hawk found that Keokuk had been made a chief. Many Sauks had believed Keokuk when he said that it was best to be friends with the Americans.

"Black Hawk is a war chief," they said. "But Keokuk is a peace chief. We want peace, not war."

Those who wanted peace formed a "peace band" and moved across the Mississippi River with Keokuk as their head chief. They settled on the banks of the Iowa River. Only 2,000 Sauks, less than half the village, were left in Saukenuk.

Black Hawk was bitter when he saw how his tribe was divided.

"Why did the Great Spirit ever send the whites to this land?" he demanded of his elders. The old men did not know. They looked at one another sadly.

Black Hawk drew his blanket across his face as a sign of sorrow. How soon would more trouble come? he wondered.

It came quickly. The British lost the war. Now Black Hawk was a defeated enemy of the Americans. They did not punish him for siding against them, but he did have to go to St. Louis to sign a peace treaty. Keokuk was at the meeting, smiling and speaking English with the white men.

Stony-faced, Black Hawk touched a quill pen to a paper he did not understand.

Keokuk had not fought in the war, but he also signed the paper. Black Hawk wondered why. But he was too proud to ask. Instead, he drew his scarlet blanket closer and walked away.

5. The Squatters Come

One day in 1816 the sound of axes rang through Saukenuk's woods. Americans were cutting trees to build the long-promised trading post on a nearby island in the Mississippi River. When it was finished, it was called Fort Armstrong. Soldiers were trained there.

"This is a strange trading post," the Sauks said.

"And we had to wait twelve years for it," Black Hawk said. He was 49 now.

But Black Hawk liked the new trader, George Davenport. He kept a good store. Often the chief sat among the piles of brightly colored blankets, talking to the American.

As the years passed, many white men pushed into Sauk land. Each spring, when the Indians returned to the village from their winter hunt, they found white families living in their lodges. Some of the Indian cornfields were fenced off. The Indian cemetery had been plowed up. If Sauk women and children went inside the fences, they were caught and whipped by the whites.

The whites would not move from the Indians' lodges until soldiers from Fort Armstrong made them go. The Indians had to camp in the woods until the soldiers came.

"How can these things happen?" Black Hawk asked George Davenport. "When the whites come into a land, they spread like a spot of raccoon grease on a new blanket. First a few whites came, and now they are everywhere."

"These people are squatters. They have no right to come here," the trader said. "The Treaty of 1804 says you may live on this land until it is opened to public settlement. Saukenuk has not been opened yet. So the soldiers drive the people away."

"Only after our cemetery had been dug up and our women beaten," Black Hawk said. "Why does the American Father allow such things?"

"The American Father has many children," replied the trader. "Some do bad things. Such children worry him, but he cannot control them. You are a chief, but you cannot control some of your Sauk children. Many buy whiskey, although you have warned them against it."

Black Hawk nodded. It was true that even a great leader could not always control his children.

Up Rock River came a long line of Sauk canoes. It was another spring. Again Saukenuk's Indians were coming home from the hunt with their loads of fine furs.

In the lead canoe Black Hawk smiled grimly. This time his family had a plan to get their lodge back from the white men without the soldiers' help.

"Everybody knows what to do," he said as Singing Bird and their children climbed from the canoe. They all loaded themselves with household goods.

A shaggy-haired white man stopped cutting wood and followed in surprise as the Indians walked into their lodge. His white wife screamed and dropped a coat she was mending. Several white children stared in wide-eyed surprise.

Singing Bird began to spread out her deerskin bed. Little Eagle hung up his father's traps. With a fierce scowl, Black Hawk took his lance and went outside. In front of the open door, he jabbed it point down in the soft earth and glared at the white family. The wife screamed again in terror. The children hid behind their mother.

"Get everything together! We'd better get out of here!" the shaggy-headed squatter shouted to his wife. Within minutes the white family had packed and fled.

Black Hawk and Singing Bird smiled at each other. "*Wach-e-ton,*" they said. "Good."

When George Davenport heard the story, he looked troubled.

"All of the Northwest Territory is being divided into states. Ohio, Indiana, and Illinois are the first ones," he told Black Hawk. "Sauk land lies in Illinois. Soon it will be opened to white settlement. Then the whites will have a right to come here. Perhaps you should move across the Mississippi River as you agreed in the Treaty of 1804."

"That treaty was not a good one. Only our subchiefs signed it."

"Later you and Keokuk and other Sauk chiefs signed a treaty too."

"That was only a peace treaty after the white man's war." Black Hawk remembered back to the day when he had touched the quill pen to paper. Did that mean he had agreed that the Sauks should move from Saukenuk? Was that why Keokuk had signed too? "That treaty didn't say that I would give away my village!" he exclaimed.

But then he saw that George Davenport thought it did mean that.

With a sinking heart, the chief told his friend, "Send a message to the American Father. Tell him we will give up all Sauk land east of the river if we can keep our village and cornfields."

George Davenport reported Black Hawk's offer. It was refused.

By summer of 1831 the American Father had lost patience with the Sauks. Why didn't they keep the terms of the treaty they'd signed 27 years ago? Well, now they must, because it was time to open the land to white settlement.

The American Father sent an order to Black Hawk: "Move out within 30 days or you will be driven out by bullets."

Black Hawk's answer was quick and angry. "This is *our* land!"

On the evening before the Sauks had to leave, 2,000 soldiers were camped outside Saukenuk. They had many guns. Black Hawk knew that tomorrow they would start to shoot. Women and children would be killed. He could not let such a thing happen.

Black Hawk walked slowly through the village. "I am beaten," he thought bitterly.

That night it rained hard. In darkness and wind, the chief led his sorrowing people from their village. By morning they had all crossed the Mississippi River to Iowa country. In their hurried flight, they had left most of their belongings behind—pots and robes, tools and traps. The corn crop, their chief food, still stood ripening in the fields. They could hunt buffalo and deer for meat,

Little Stabbing Chief the Younger,
a brave

Roaring Thunder,
Black Hawk's son

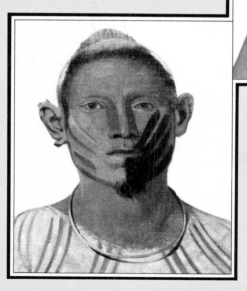

The Iowa, a brave

BLACK HAWK'S PEOPLE

George Catlin, an American artist, traveled through Indian country in the early 1800s. In over 600 portraits and landscape paintings, he recorded Indian life with great feeling and accuracy. Below are some of Catlin's paintings of Black Hawk's people.

Soup, adviser to Black Hawk

The Swimmer, a brave

but without corn there would not be enough to eat.

Winter came. The people shivered in their make-shift camp and remembered the warm blankets they had left in Saukenuk.

Neapope, one of Black Hawk's best warriors, went back across the river to visit the friendly Winnebagoes. They were a small tribe who lived in northern Illinois and Wisconsin. They, too, were having trouble with the American Father.

In a short time Neapope returned. He said that if Black Hawk led his warriors to fight for Saukenuk, the British Father in Canada would send him war supplies.

"How do you know?" Black Hawk asked.

"The Winnebagoes' wise man told me," answered Neapope.

Black Hawk didn't know what to do. He was 64 years old, the "old chief" now. He was tired. His people needed food, not war.

Then the Winnebagoes sent a messenger to Black Hawk. He said that next spring the Sauks could come and plant a corn crop on Winnebago land. The Winnebagoes would provide seed and tools.

"In the spring!" the hungry Sauks told one another. "In the spring we will plant again!" The words tasted as sweet as new corn in their mouths.

6. Black Hawk's War

Under a blue April sky, Black Hawk's 2,000 Sauks came to the Mississippi. The cruel winter was over. Now the sun shone warm on their backs, and soon they would be among their Winnebago friends. Black Hawk smiled broadly as he rode his white pony along the water's edge. Everywhere there was bustle and noise.

"*Wach-e-ton. Wach-e-ton.* Good. Good," he said as he watched the women, children, and old people start off in the canoes. The women were singing a Sauk planting song.

"*Wach-e-ton,*" Black Hawk said as his whooping warriors guided their horses out into the river.

At last he turned his own horse into the water. Yes, it was good to be going back toward home. *Wach-e-ton!*

All the way across the river, the women sang their song. At the place where Rock River flows into the Mississippi, the canoes turned up the Rock. Suddenly the singing stopped. In the distance where the lodges of Saukenuk had stood, there was nothing! Every Sauk knew at once what had happened. The soldiers had burned down Saukenuk.

Saukenuk's women sat in silent grief as they passed the ashes of their homes.

117

It was 35 miles up Rock River to Prophet's Town in Winnebago country. Here almost a thousand Indians from many tribes lived, close to the Prophet, a medicine man, or "wise man." The Indians believed that the Prophet talked to *Man-ee-do*, the Great Spirit.

When the Sauks arrived, he came to the riverbank to greet them. He was a tall man in a fringed deerskin suit with beads around his neck.

"You sent us a message that we could come here and grow corn," Black Hawk said.

The Prophet brushed the words aside. "The Great Spirit wants you to drive the white men from the Rock River valley," he declared. "Warriors from many tribes will join you. The British Father will send you guns and ammunition, food and clothing."

"We have come to plant corn," Black Hawk said.

The Prophet's eyes flashed angrily. "Are you dogs, that you should slink away when the white man is near? If you are men, you must obey my words! The Great Spirit commands it!"

Black Hawk listened and pondered. He had held out against the whites for many years, yet Saukenuk lay in ashes. But if the Great Spirit promised success in war, the village might be rebuilt.

"I would like to get our land back," he told the Prophet. "We will talk about it while the women plant corn."

The corn was never planted. There was no time. Governor Reynolds of Illinois soon learned that the Sauks had returned, and he grew very fearful.

"It is an invasion!" he cried. Quickly he sent out a call for 1,600 men to form troops to march against the Indians.

Across the Illinois prairie, the words swept like wildfire: "The Indians are on the warpath!"

Soon the new troops gathered at Fort Armstrong. Some started after Black Hawk on horseback. Others went by boat up the Rock and the Mississippi rivers. Winnebago spies brought the news to Black Hawk.

"We cannot fight such an army!" the chief declared. "We must get our women and children back across the Great River before the soldiers find us."

Before Black Hawk could make his plans, a scouting party of 300 soldiers camped one night at a place called Sycamore Creek. They did not know that 40 Sauks were nearby, having a meal of dog meat.

When Black Hawk heard about the camp, he said, "I will talk to their chief and explain that we are peaceable and want only to take our families across the river." He sent some braves to the soldiers' camp. The braves carried a white flag of truce.

The troopers had little army training. They had never been in a battle and knew nothing of the rules of war. When they saw the Indians, they became excited. They rushed for their horses and rode at the startled Indians, shooting their guns. Two Sauks fell from their ponies, dead.

Black Hawk had been watching from a cotton-wood grove.

He gasped when he saw his truce bearers shot down. Such an act against men carrying a white flag was unheard of!

Furiously he shouted the war cry and led his warriors in attack.

The troopers turned and fled. In their panic some of them threw away their guns. The Sauks chased them until darkness fell, and they killed twelve of them.

"Now it is war!" Black Hawk told his people.

He led them into the deep woods where they could hide from the soldiers until help came from other tribes. Then he called his warriors around him.

"We must avenge our murdered truce bearers!" he told them. He sent the warriors out in small bands to raid the countryside.

Fierce in war paint and feathers, they attacked lonely cabins and farmhouses. They burned and killed. Soon Black Hawk's name was feared all over Illinois.

Governor Reynolds sent out a call for 2,000 more men to help in the fight. Army camps were soon filled with new soldiers learning to march and drill. They did not know that Black Hawk's war would end before many of them had finished their training. One such soldier was a young store-keeper from New Salem whose name was Abraham Lincoln.

Spring turned to summer, but no warriors from other tribes came to join Black Hawk. The British Father sent no supplies. At last the chief realized his Sauks must fight alone.

"The Prophet's words were false!" he said angrily. "Nobody planned to join us, and the Great Spirit gave no commands. The Prophet only wanted to stir up trouble."

Scouting parties drew close to Black Hawk's camp. The Indians had to move. Little by little they were driven far north into Wisconsin country. Spies reported that the Americans had 3,000 troops. Black Hawk had 500 warriors. With them were 1,500 women, children, and old people. They had little ammunition and food.

Late on a rainy July afternoon, the desperate

Sauks came to a spot on the Wisconsin River called Wisconsin Heights. They were worn out and weak from hunger. Many were sick. But they had to go on.

"We will cross the river here," Black Hawk told them.

The warriors began to take the women and children to an island in the river.

Suddenly a lookout shouted to them, "Soldiers are coming!"

Black Hawk ordered in a clear, loud voice, "Braves, follow me and attack!"

A few braves stayed behind to help the women and children. The rest rode back from the river to fight the soldiers. Guns barked, and bullets ripped through the rain.

The battle was hard and bloody. When it was over, 68 Indians lay dead in the tall, wet grass. Others were dying. When darkness fell, the soldiers withdrew to tend their wounded. Under cover of night, Black Hawk and his braves slipped away to join the rest of their band waiting on the other side of the river.

As the sorrowful Indians trudged through the rain, the old chief's heart ached.

"Once we were as happy as the buffalo on the plains. Now we are as miserable as the hungry, howling wolf on the prairie," he thought.

7. Battle of the Bad Axe

In a few days soldiers were on the Indians' trail again. It was an easy trail to follow.

Along the way lay the bodies of Sauks who had died from wounds or starvation. There were bones from horses the Indians had eaten. There were trees from which they had stripped the bark for food.

At last the pitiful band came to the place where the Bad Axe River flows into the Mississippi. They had only three canoes.

Warriors used their hatchets to chop down small swamp oaks to build a raft. Women gathered long strands of grass and twisted them into ropes to tie the logs together. Then the raft was loaded with women and children.

As the braves pushed it out into the current of the Mississippi, the women gave a great cry. They pointed up the river. There, coming slowly toward them, was the American army steamer, *Warrior*.

Quickly Black Hawk tied a white rag onto the end of a stick. As the *Warrior* stopped in mid-river, Black Hawk waved his flag of truce.

"I am Black Hawk," he called. "We want to surrender. Send a boat for me so that I can talk to your war chief."

On the *Warrior* Captain Throckmorton turned to

The Battle of the Bad Axe, where the water ran red with the blood of Black Hawk's people.

a man who knew how to speak Indian languages. "What is the Indian saying?" When told, he said, "Tell the Indians to come here in their own boat if they want to talk."

"We have no canoes," shouted Black Hawk in answer. He pointed to the river where the Sauks' three canoes were far across carrying women and children.

Suddenly three rounds of cannon fire came from the boat. The deadly fire tore through a group of Indians standing near their chief. Several fell dying to the ground.

With a howl of rage, Black Hawk threw down his white flag.

Then from shore and boat rattled the fierce fire of guns. On the boat a white man was wounded. On shore 23 Indians were killed.

Later Captain Throckmorton would explain that he had heard many tales about Black Hawk, and he thought the Indian probably had warriors hidden, waiting to attack. That, he said, was why he ignored the white flag.

The *Warrior* was short of fuel. It moved on. Night fell. In the darkness the Sauks got a few more women and children across the Mississippi River.

The first pink rays of dawn shone on a long line of American mounted troops. They were riding toward the shore where the starving Indians were gathered. A bugle shrilled ATTACK! The troopers began shooting.

The braves fought back, dodging from tree to tree. They tried to hold off the soldiers while their families escaped. Women plunged into the river with their children on their backs. Many drowned. Many others were killed by bullets.

The *Warrior* returned. Her flag flapped in the morning breeze. The sun shone on her polished cannon. And from her deck riflemen shot over the river, picking off swimmers trying to cross to safety.

The Battle of the Bad Axe lasted three hours.

Near the end Black Hawk jumped on his white pony and fled into the woods. There was nothing now he could do for his people. Most of them had been killed. Of the 2,000 Sauks who had crossed the Mississippi in April to plant corn, only a few hundred would live to get back to the Iowa country.

For several weeks Black Hawk hid in the woods. A few other Sauks who had escaped joined him.

One evening, peering from the brush, he saw a young American sitting on a stone watching the sunset. He was Robert Grignon, a trader whom Black Hawk knew.

The old chief walked into the open.

Startled, the American jumped up. Then he smiled in greeting.

Black Hawk said he wanted to surrender.

"I am hunted down like a deer by dogs," the chief said. "The forests are full of men who seek my body dead or alive. I will go to the American agent and give myself up, as a man should do. Flight is useless, and I want no more fighting.

"But I will be shot if I am seen by the spies or soldiers, for he who kills me gets a reward."

"That is true," the young man said. "When you go to the fort to surrender, you must travel by back roads and take great care."

Black Hawk nodded. His little band of Sauks

came from the woods. They told Grignon good-bye and set out by back trails for the Wisconsin fort at Prairie du Chien many miles away.

On the morning of August 27, 1832, Black Hawk and his followers walked into the fort and gave themselves up. With them were two Winnebago warriors, Chaetar and One-Eyed Decorah. The Winnebagoes said they had captured Black Hawk, and they wanted the reward of 20 ponies that had been offered for him. Black Hawk said nothing. Let his friends get all the ponies they could from the white men!

Black Hawk was 65 years old, worn and battle weary. He was sad at the memory of his people's defeat. He was a prisoner with handcuffs on his wrists. Yet he walked proudly, as a chief should, when the white soldiers led him to their jail.

8. Proud Prisoner

In chains, Black Hawk was sent to the prison at Jefferson Barracks near Saint Louis.

"My warriors have fallen around me," he told his captors. "I see my evil day at hand. I am a prisoner of the white man, but I have done nothing of which to be ashamed. I have fought the battles of my people against the white men

127

Black Hawk and his son. "We have buried the tomahawk," the brave old chief said, "and the sound of the rifle will hereafter only bring death to the deer and the buffalo. . . ."

who came year after year to cheat us and take away our land."

In the spring of 1833, President Andrew Jackson had Chief Black Hawk brought to Washington, D.C. The president wanted to make sure that the chief understood how strong the white men were.

Black Hawk was a prisoner. He had no power. But his name was still honored by his people and by Indians of other tribes who did not like the whites. President Jackson did not want Black Hawk to encourage any more Indian uprisings.

One fine April day they faced each other in the president's office in the White House.

Both men were nearing 70; both were warriors who had known great danger. "He has seen as many winters as I have and seems to be a great brave," Black Hawk thought.

Black Hawk was not afraid of the president. Instead, he liked him! They were two old lions who understood each other.

President Jackson told Black Hawk that he was to be taken on a tour of some United States cities. The president said, "You will see the strength of the white people. You will see that we have as many young men as there are leaves in the woods. What can you do against us? Bury the hatchet and live in peace with your white brothers."

"We did not want to conquer the whites," Black Hawk replied. "We took up the hatchet to revenge injuries which my people could no longer stand. That is why I fought. Now the hatchet is buried."

Black Hawk was held in jail at Fortress Monroe in Virginia for a short time. Then he was taken on a tour of Baltimore, Philadelphia, and New York City. Thousands of people came to see him. They were surprised to find that he was a kindly man.

Then Black Hawk was allowed to go back west to live on a small reservation in the Iowa country, where Singing Bird and his children waited for him. There he died on October 3, 1838, when he was 71. He was buried in a military uniform given to him by President Jackson.

Although he was defeated in life, in death Black Hawk was honored even by his enemies.

High on a bluff overlooking the Rock River valley, the land of his fathers, stands a huge stone statue of Black Hawk. It represents the proud spirit of this brave warrior.

But Black Hawk's own words are his best memorial. He said, "Rock River was a beautiful country. I liked my town, my cornfields, and the home of my people. I fought for them."

Those are the words of Black Hawk, war chief of the Sauks, a great patriot who struggled mightily to save his nation.

About Black Hawk's People

The Sauk Indians were a brave and independent people who lived along the Mississippi River in Wisconsin, Illinois, and Iowa. In the summer they made their homes in villages such as Saukenuk. Here the women grew corn and other crops, while the men hunted in the forests or fished nearby. After the harvest the entire village moved to the hunting grounds to trap beaver and other small animals. The fur of these animals was traded for pots, pans, guns, and traps. The map below shows the route Black Hawk's band took from Fort Madison to the mouth of the Bad Axe River, where the final battle of Black Hawk's War was fought.

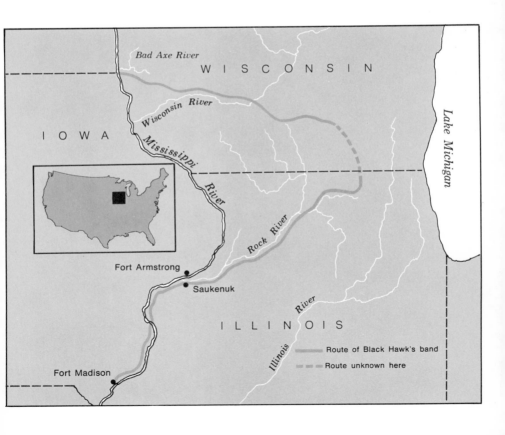

Osceola

Seminole War Chief

by Wyatt Blassingame

You have guns and so have we. You have powder
and lead, and so have we. Your men will fight,
and so will ours, till the last drop of Seminole
blood has moistened the dust of his hunting
ground!

Osceola

133

1. This Is My Home

The Indian boy let his canoe drift quietly. His eyes were on the bend of the river close ahead. A deer stood there, its front feet at the water's edge. Its head was lowered to drink.

At first the boy did not move. Then slowly, carefully, he reached for his bow. At the same time the deer raised its head. It saw the boy, turned, and disappeared among the bushes.

The boy smiled. It did not matter that the deer had got away. There was plenty of meat in his village.

He let the canoe continue to drift. The river was narrow here. The water was dark, but when he looked straight down into it, it was clear as glass. The grass growing on the bottom moved with the current of the river as if blown by wind.

Now the boy picked up his paddle. He sent the canoe gliding to a willow tree that overhung the water. A fishing line was tied to one of the limbs. When the boy pulled up the line, there was a fish on the end of it.

The boy smiled happily. He took the fish off the hook and put it in the canoe. He put a worm on the hook and dropped it back into the water. "Maybe there will be another fish later," he thought. "This is a good place, a good river. Florida is a good land."

The boy could still remember a time before he had come to Florida. He had lived somewhere to the north, probably in what is now Alabama. That had been a good place too. But white men who called themselves Americans had wanted the Indian lands. For a long time there had been war. White soldiers had driven the Indians from one place to another. Finally the boy with his mother and a few other Indians had come here—to Florida. They wanted to live in peace.

The Americans didn't own Florida. They said it belonged to Spain. The Indian boy didn't know where Spain was. He was sure that Florida belonged to his own people, the Seminole Indians.

Slowly the canoe drifted downstream. Soon the boy could see the low hill where the Seminole village stood. Then he heard men shouting. Their voices were angry. One man was waving a gun over his head.

The boy left his canoe at the riverbank and ran toward the village. There were only a few houses, called "chickees." The chickees had wooden floors and roofs made of palm leaves, but no walls. On the ground between the chickees were the open cook fires of the families.

The women were busily working near the fires. One of them was the boy's mother. "What has happened?" he asked.

She looked at him with fear in her eyes. "An Indian came while you were gone. He brought bad news."

"What is it?"

"White men say this land now belongs to the Americans. Spain has sold it to them."

"The Americans?" Now he thought again of the

Osceola grew up in Florida, where the climate permitted Seminoles to live in open chickees.

time of wars, when his people had been driven from place to place. "Will their soldiers come?" he asked. "Will they drive us away?"

"I don't know," his mother answered sadly.

The boy turned. Slowly he walked past the chickees to the edge of the low hill. Oak trees grew all around him. Spanish moss hung in long streamers from their limbs. Beyond the trees he could see the river. On the other side of the river was a swamp. The strange, twisted roots of cypress trees rose above the dark water. A great blue heron stood at the edge of the trees.

"This is *my* home," the boy thought. "I will not let anyone drive me away from it. Not ever."

2. Meeting at Fort King

Seminole Indians often changed their names as they grew from boys into men. The childhood name of the Seminole boy who vowed he would never give up his home is not known. But thirteen years later, when he was a young man, his name was Osceola. On October 22, 1832, Osceola stood quietly under the moss-hung oak trees outside Fort King. He listened while General Wiley Thompson made a speech.

Osceola did not like General Thompson. He knew the general's job was to get the Seminoles to give up their homes and move west of the Mississippi River. Once again white men wanted more of the Indians' land.

Osceola listened carefully while the general spoke. "In the past," General Thompson said, "your chiefs have all promised to leave Florida peacefully. You have always broken your promise. Now the Great Father in Washington grows weary of waiting. You must leave right away."

Osceola looked at Micanopy, the head chief of the Seminoles. Micanopy was an old man. He did not want to leave Florida, but he did not want war. He sat with his head bowed.

"I must have your answer," the general said. "Right now."

The old chief started to speak. As he did, Osceola stepped quickly to his side. He leaned over and whispered, "Tell him you cannot answer now. Tell him you must talk with all the other chiefs first."

Micanopy nodded. "I must meet with all of the other chiefs," he told General Thompson. "Tomorrow we will give you our answer." He stood up. Followed by Osceola and the other Indians, he left the fort.

Fort King belonged to the Americans but it was not much of a fort. There were a few wooden buildings for soldiers inside a high fence. Outside the fence were a few more buildings. One of these was a small store that sold goods to the Indians and to the few settlers who lived nearby. Another was the home and office of General Thompson.

That night the general left his house and went into the fort. He was angry. "When the Indians met this afternoon I had a spy among them," he told the soldiers. "The spy tells me that most of the chiefs were willing to leave Florida. But now Osceola is trying to change their minds."

A young officer asked, "Is Osceola a leading chief?"

"He isn't a chief at all," General Thompson said, "not by birth anyway. I don't know who his father was. Some people say he was a white man named Powell. Osceola says his father was an Indian. If so, he may have been killed while fighting the settlers in Alabama or Georgia. That's where Osceola used to live."

"But Osceola is a Seminole, isn't he?" the officer asked.

"Seminoles are not really a single tribe," General Thompson explained. "Most of the original Florida Indians were killed or died of disease years ago. Other Indians moved here from Alabama and Georgia. Some came to get away from the white men. Some came to get away from other Indians they had been fighting. Seminole means 'one who has broken away' or 'runaway.' So all the Indians who have moved to Florida may be called Seminoles. They live in small bands with many different chiefs."

"If Osceola is not a chief, how can he have much influence over the men who are?"

"Osceola is very clever," General Thompson said. "He is a natural leader. But I think that the real chiefs will agree to leave Florida, no matter what Osceola may say."

3. Signed with a Knife

As General Thompson had explained, Osceola was not a chief by birth. But he was intelligent and brave. Many of the young Indians wanted him for their leader.

When the chiefs met again with General Thompson, Osceola was with them. The Indians sat in a row on the ground. Jumper and Charley Amathla and many others were there for the meeting. Micanopy sat in the center. Close beside him was Osceola.

General Thompson did not look at Osceola. He looked at the old chief. "What is your answer?" he asked.

Micanopy spoke slowly. "Eleven years ago the Seminoles signed a treaty with the white men at a place you call Moultrie Creek. In this treaty we gave up much of our land. In return the Great Father in Washington promised we should keep the land left to us. This is the treaty we wish to live by. We do not want to leave our homes."

"You have signed other treaties since then," General Thompson said. "Two years ago at Payne's Landing you signed a promise to leave Florida. But you have not gone. Now you must go."

The general's words made Osceola angry. He looked at Micanopy, but the old chief sat with his head bowed. The other chiefs also were uncertain how to answer the general.

Osceola leaped to his feet. "That treaty at Payne's Landing was a white man's trick. The white man has broken more promises to the Seminoles than there are raindrops in a storm. We will never leave our homes. Never!"

The general's face turned red, but he controlled his anger. "I speak only to the chiefs," he said, "not to some unknown troublemaker." He turned to Micanopy. "What is your answer?"

"Osceola speaks for his people," the old chief said. "We do not wish to leave our homes."

After this meeting more and more Seminoles wanted Osceola for their leader. Micanopy was very old. Charley Amathla was an important chief, but he was timid. Osceola had sworn he

Osceola refuses to sign a treaty which demands that the Seminoles move from their homes at once.

would never give up his home. The young warriors knew he would keep his word to them.

Soon General Thompson called the Indians to another meeting. He spread a large sheet of paper on a wooden table. It was a new treaty. The treaty stated that the Seminoles would agree to leave Florida at once. Then General Thompson read them a letter from President Andrew Jackson.

The president said that if the Seminoles did not go peacefully, his soldiers would force them to leave.

"You have heard the Great Father's words," General Thompson said. "You must sign the treaty."

Osceola did not move, but slowly, one after

another, some of the chiefs went to the table. None of them could write his name. Instead the chiefs made cross marks on the paper. General Thompson was smiling. He looked at Osceola. "Since you act like a chief, sign the treaty."

Osceola walked to the table. His lips were tight. His dark eyes flashed as he looked at the general. Suddenly he pulled a knife from his belt and stabbed it through the paper. "This is the only way I will sign a treaty with the white man!" he cried.

4. In Chains

About a month later Osceola visited the store at Fort King. The storekeeper was named Rogers. Rogers refused to sell Osceola powder and lead for his gun. "General Thompson has given me orders not to sell any more powder to Indians," he said.

"How does the general expect us to kill game for food?" Osceola asked. "Does he want the Indians to starve?"

Rogers laughed. "Maybe he doesn't care about you."

Angrily, Osceola walked across the clearing to General Thompson's office. There he and the general began to argue. The argument became violent. Finally Osceola turned on his heel and walked out.

The general turned to four soldiers who were standing nearby. "Arrest that Indian!" he ordered.

The soldiers ran after Osceola who was walking across the clearing. His head was high, his face hard with anger. "You are now under arrest," one soldier said.

Osceola did not look at him. He kept walking. Two of the soldiers grabbed him by the arms.

Osceola was not a big man, but he was as quick and strong as a panther. He broke away from the two men who held him. When he did, the other two jumped on him. But holding Osceola was like holding a wildcat. In an instant all five men were rolling on the ground. Other soldiers came running. Finally they carried Osceola, still fighting, into the fort. They chained him to the wall.

For four hours Osceola fought fiercely. Then, suddenly, he stopped struggling. He sat there motionless. The chains on his ankles and wrists were bloodstained where they had cut into his flesh. But Osceola felt no pain. He felt only shame and anger—hotter than any he had ever known.

That night some food was brought to Osceola. He did not even look at it. He looked at the chains that held him—the chains put on him by white men.

Unless he could escape he might, like other Indians, be sent west of the Mississippi. But he could not break the chains, so he planned how he could escape another way.

The next morning Osceola sent for Charley Amathla and several other Indians. "Go to the general," he said. "Tell him that if I am set free, I will sign the treaty."

The chiefs did just as Osceola asked. When they had gone, General Thompson went to the fort. "If you sign the treaty here alone," he told Osceola, "none of your people will know. Once you are free, you can tell them you did not sign."

"I do not tell them lies," Osceola said.

"I want your people to see you sign," General Thompson said. "I will set you free if you will give me your word to return in five days. Bring your people with you to see you sign."

"I give my word," Osceola said.

Just as he had promised, Osceola returned five days later. With him were 79 Indians. Like most Seminoles, Osceola had two wives. They came with him, carrying his two small sons. The young warriors who had chosen Osceola as their leader came also. Silently they watched Osceola make an X on the paper.

This mark meant nothing to Osceola. He had promised to make it, and he had made it. He had gone freely to General Thompson, and the general had put him in chains. Now he had escaped in the only way he could. But he would not leave his homeland willingly. Ever!

5. Death to Traitors

Osceola now lived in a village not far from Fort King. The village was on a low hill with big, moss-hung oak trees. There were a few chickees with cook fires between them. From each fire logs stuck out like the spokes of a wheel. These logs served as seats. When more wood was needed for the fire, the burning end of a log could be pushed closer to the center.

Here in the summer of 1835 the Seminoles held a secret meeting. Dressed in their long fringed shirts, with egret plumes in their hair, the warriors sat around one of the fires. The light flickered on their dark faces and on the barrels of their guns. One after another the chiefs stood up to speak.

"I do not want to leave my home," one chief said. "But if the Seminoles do not leave, the white soldiers will start war. We cannot defeat them in battle. We are too few in number, with too few guns. General Thompson has told us we must bring our cattle to Fort King. We must sell them to the white man. Then we must go to the place called Fort Brooke on Tampa Bay. From there the white man's ships will carry us west. I do not want to go, but we have no choice."

Another chief agreed with the first, and then another. Now Osceola spoke. "White men have always driven the Indian from one home to another," he said. "If we move west, the white men will drive us from there. Finally we will be driven into the sea to drown. If I must die, I will die at home. Florida is my home. I will not leave it."

Osceola's fierce spirit inspired the other Indians. When a vote was taken, they agreed they would refuse to leave Florida. Now they would look on any Seminole as a traitor if he sold his cattle and planned to leave. As a traitor, he would have to be killed.

Not all the Seminoles were at this meeting. Some had already moved close to Fort Brooke to wait for the white man's ships. Others were planning to do so. One of these was the chief, Charley Amathla.

When the chiefs who had met with Osceola heard that Charley Amathla was about to sell his cattle, they held another meeting. Charley Amathla, they said, must be killed as a traitor. It must be done as soon as possible.

Next day Osceola and twelve warriors hid beside the path that led from Charley Amathla's village to Fort King. They had learned that the chief had driven his cattle to Fort King that morning. Soon he would be coming back to his home.

Osceola felt no shame and no sorrow for what he was about to do. Charley Amathla had joined the white men. He was an enemy at war. Osceola was a soldier doing his job.

In the late afternoon Charley Amathla came down the path. When he was close, Osceola gave the signal. The warriors sprang to their feet. No one spoke. Thirteen guns fired all at once. Charley Amathla fell.

"Look," one of the warriors said. From beside the fallen man he picked up a small bag of gold pieces. "This is the money the white men paid him for his cattle."

"Give it to me," Osceola said. He flung the gold on the ground beside Charley Amathla's body. "Let us leave it there," he said, "so everyone will know what the white man's gold has bought."

6. Revenge

The Seminole War began. Before it was over, it would be the longest and bloodiest of all the Indian wars in American history.

All across Florida, bands of Indians began to raid the farms of settlers. Sometimes they killed the people and burned their houses. Sometimes they were driven off by the settlers' guns.

Osceola took little part in these raids. "I do not make war on women and children," he said. "I make war only on soldiers."

Osceola knew that to defeat the white soldiers, his people would need more guns, lead, and powder. The only way to get these supplies was to take them from the soldiers.

A scout brought Osceola word that three army

Seminole Indian warriors fire on a sloop from an ambush on the shore.

supply wagons were moving from one fort to another. There were only a few soldiers assigned to guard the wagons.

With 80 braves, Osceola raced through the woods. They hid beside the road over which the wagons would travel. "Wait until I give the war whoop," Osceola said. "Then fire."

Hidden by a palmetto thicket, he watched the wagons come closer. A few soldiers rode ahead, a few more behind. Suddenly Osceola's voice rang out, high and thin and terrible. The Indians' guns fired. Some of the soldiers fell dead, others ran.

While the Indians were unloading the wagons, some more soldiers arrived. Their captain ordered a charge. He expected the Indians to run. Instead, they hid in the palmettos and fired back. Outnumbered, the soldiers had to retreat. Osceola and his warriors took everything they could use from the wagons, then they set them on fire. In time, still more soldiers arrived, but the Indians had disappeared.

Osceola had never forgotten that he had been put in chains by General Thompson. Carefully, Osceola made plans for his revenge. However, it was not revenge alone he wanted. If he could capture Fort King, he could get guns and food for his people.

On the morning of December 28, 1835, Osceola and his warriors surrounded the fort. They lay hidden in the thick woods, watching. Osceola knew he could not capture the fort except by surprise. He must get inside the high fence.

The commander of the fort did not know the Indians were near. All day he kept his soldiers working on the fence to make it stronger. There was never a time the Indians could cross the clearing without being seen.

In the late afternoon General Thompson and a soldier named Lieutenant Smith left the general's office. They started across the clearing toward Rogers's store. The store was close to the woods where Osceola lay hidden.

Quickly Osceola made his plan. He waited until General Thompson and Lieutenant Smith were within gun range. Then Osceola's terrible war whoop rang out. From all along the edge of the woods, guns fired. General Thompson and Lieutenant Smith fell dead.

Swiftly, Osceola and some of his warriors rushed to Rogers's store. They killed the storekeeper and two clerks. But they did not find the guns and powder Osceola hoped for. These had already been moved inside the fort.

From the store the Indians raced back to the woods. Once more they hid and waited. Osceola knew the soldiers inside the fort had heard the shooting. He hoped that the commander would order them to rush outside and learn what had happened. The gate in the high fence might be left open. Then the Seminoles could charge in and capture the fort.

The commander kept the gate closed. When Osceola saw he could not capture the fort, he led his warriors back into the forest. Behind him lay the body of the man who had once ordered him put in chains.

7. Battle of the Withlacoochee

On the same day that Osceola killed General Thompson, other Seminoles were fighting another battle.

Major Francis Dade was marching from Fort Brooke toward Fort King with a hundred soldiers. They were ambushed by the Seminoles. All but three soldiers were killed. Dade State Park is now located on the site of the battle.

After this battle Chiefs Micanopy, Jumper, and Alligator led their warriors to a place called the Cove of the Withlacoochee. This was a swampy place with many island-dotted lakes and narrow streams. It was about half land, half water. A person could be lost here very easily. Osceola and his followers soon joined the other Indians at the Cove of the Withlacoochee.

At this time the American soldiers in Florida were commanded by General Duncan Clinch. His spies told him where the Indians were gathering. With a force of about 700 men he marched toward the Cove of the Withlacoochee.

An Indian scout saw the soldiers. He raced to tell the chiefs that the soldiers were coming.

The chiefs could not agree what to do. Some wanted to go deeper into the swamps and hide. Some wanted to fight where they were. "Before the soldiers can reach us," Osceola said, "they must cross the Withlacoochee River. We must wait there for them. When some soldiers are on one side of the river, some on the other, we can attack."

Chief Alligator agreed with him. He and Osceola took 250 warriors and hurried to the place where the trail crossed the river. There they hid behind trees and palmetto thickets.

Osceola was wearing a blue coat. It had belonged to one of the soldiers who was killed with Major Dade.

Several hours passed. Where were the troops? Could they have slipped past?

Osceola sent scouts to look. Soon one of them came running back. General Clinch's men had lost the trail in the woods. They had reached the river two miles downstream from the ford. At that point the river was too deep to wade. But the soldiers had found an old canoe. They were crossing the river in it, a few men at a time.

Quickly Osceola led the Indians downstream. Soon they could see the soldiers. Some were trying to build a bridge of logs. One man was paddling the canoe back and forth. He would pick up six soldiers on the north bank and take them to the south bank. Then he would paddle back for more. About two hundred soldiers had already crossed.

Osceola told his warriors to slip through the trees and surround the soldiers on the south bank. Before they could do this, someone shouted, "Indians!" Both sides opened fire.

Most of the Indians were hidden along the edge of a swamp. The soldiers were in a small clearing near the riverbank. These were well-trained army regulars. When General Clinch ordered a charge, they rushed at the swamp. Their bayonets gleamed in the sunlight.

Osceola ordered his men to fade back into the swamp, shooting as they went. The soldiers did not want to follow the Seminoles into the swamp. They returned to the clearing. Now Osceola shouted for his men to advance. Once more they fired on the troops caught in the open.

Time and again the soldiers saw the flash of Osceola's blue coat. They heard his war cry. A bullet struck Osceola in the hand, but he kept on fighting.

Soon many of the soldiers on the south bank were killed or wounded. General Clinch ordered his men to retreat. They hurried over the crude bridge that had been finished during the fighting. The Seminoles had won the battle.

That night there was much singing and dancing in the Cove of the Withlacoochee. Osceola sang and danced with the others, but his mind was busy. He knew that when one soldier was killed, ten others might take his place. One victory did not win a war.

8. Sickness at Fort Drane

As the Seminole War went on, President Jackson sent more and more soldiers into Florida. They built new forts along the trails. From these forts they marched against the small Indian villages.

The Seminoles did not have enough men or guns to defeat the soldiers in open battle. They could only fight briefly, then retreat into the swamps. They took their women and children with them, leaving their towns empty. The soldiers captured and burned Osceola's town. They burned the towns of Micanopy, Jumper, and other chiefs who would not agree to leave Florida. In turn, the Seminoles burned the homes of settlers. They attacked any small bands of soldiers they found outside of the forts.

At a place called Fort Drane, many of the troops became ill with malaria. The commanding officer died. Others were too sick to fight. The able soldiers, carrying the sick with them, moved to another fort.

Osceola did not know why the Americans had left Fort Drane. He did not know that malaria had swept the fort. As soon as the Americans left, Osceola and his followers moved into the fort.

Soon Osceola became sick. First he felt cold, even in the hottest sunshine. His whole body shook as if he were freezing. Then, strangely, he began to feel hot. He burned with a high fever. Sometimes he felt as if he were floating in space. He could not think clearly.

After a few hours the fever passed and Osceola felt well again. But a few days later he had another attack, and then another. He would never be really well again.

One day an Indian scout came racing into Fort Drane. He told Osceola there were soldiers only a few miles away. They were going to attack.

Quickly Osceola called everyone inside the fort.

The warriors took their places behind the high fence that surrounded the buildings. Only a few of them had guns. But the fence would protect them, Osceola thought. Firing from behind it, they could hold off the soldiers.

The soldiers, however, did not charge the fort. Instead, they opened fire with one small cannon. The cannonballs knocked down part of the fence. The balls smashed into the buildings, killing men and women.

Osceola and all his warriors fought bravely, but they could not stand against the cannon. Osceola told the women and children to slip away on the far side of the fort. There was a swamp close by. The women and children disappeared into it. When they were safe, Osceola and his warriors slipped away too.

9. Kidnapped

All that fall and winter the Seminoles were hunted like animals. They traveled in small bands. Wherever they went, the white soldiers followed. Often the soldiers used bloodhounds to track down the Indians. They drove them from their villages and burned the chickees. They killed many of the warriors and captured many women and children.

Those who were captured were sent west. Those

who escaped fled to new hiding places. There was no time to plant gardens. The Indians were always hungry. Many of them had no clothes.

Osceola was sick much of the time now. But between the spells of chills and fever, his head was as clear as ever. He knew now that the Seminoles could never defeat the soldiers. He wanted peace. He had never been in favor of war except to defend his home country. But he would not surrender.

Several times Osceola sent messages to the army generals. Sometimes he met with them himself under a white flag of truce. Osceola promised that if his people could stay in Florida, they would end the war.

Each time the generals refused. There could be no peace until all the Seminoles moved west.

By the summer of 1837 most of the Seminole chiefs were ready to surrender. Their people were starving. They had little powder or lead for their guns.

In despair Micanopy, Jumper, and other chiefs led their people to Fort Brooke. Before long, 700 Seminoles were camped near the fort. General Thomas Jesup was now commanding the soldiers. He sent for ships from New Orleans to carry the Indians west.

Osceola had not gone to Fort Brooke. Instead,

he and a chief named Arpeika met in a swamp somewhere in central Florida. Both men were thin from lack of food. Fever had sunk Osceola's eyes deep in his face. "If Micanopy, Jumper, and their bands leave Florida," Osceola said, "we will not have enough men left to fight."

"How can we stop them?" Arpeika asked.

"If Micanopy were to disappear, his people would not wait for the ships. They would go back to the swamps."

Arpeika looked at Osceola. "How do we make the old chief disappear?"

"How many warriors do we have?"

Arpeika thought awhile. "With yours and mine . . . about 200."

"That will be enough," Osceola said. "Micanopy's braves will not want to fight us."

A few nights later Osceola, Arpeika, and their warriors slipped out of the trees near the fort and into Micanopy's camp. They went quietly to the chickee where the old chief slept. They shook him awake. "Come," Osceola said.

Chief Micanopy knew why they were there. "No," he said, "I have given my word to General Jesup."

Osceola gave a signal. Four strong warriors grabbed the old chief. They put him on a horse and led him away from camp. Other warriors

Osceola led his people in what was to be the
longest and fiercest of all of the Indian wars.

captured Chief Jumper the same way. The chiefs were not hurt, but they were taken away from Fort Brooke.

The next morning all the Seminoles who were camped near the fort learned what had happened. Without their leaders they did what Osceola had expected them to do. They slipped away from the camp and disappeared into the forest.

10. Captured

General Thomas Jesup was furious when he learned Micanopy and Jumper had been kidnapped. He ordered his soldiers to chase the Seminoles harder than ever. In the next few months many Indians were killed or captured.

Osceola and his band traveled across Florida. They hid in a swamp near St. Augustine. Many were starving. Some, like Osceola, were sick much of the time.

The general in command at St. Augustine was named Joseph Hernandez. Osceola sent him a peace pipe and a white egret plume. Along with these, he sent a message saying he wished to talk under a flag of truce.

General Jesup was in St. Augustine at this time. So he ordered General Hernandez to meet Osceola. If Osceola refused to surrender, General Jesup said, the Indians were to be captured in spite of the flag of truce.

On the day of October 21, 1837, General Hernandez and a few officers rode toward Osceola's camp. They could see the white flag flying from a tall pole. Beneath the flag stood Osceola. With him were thirteen other chiefs and seventy-one warriors.

Osceola looked thin and sick. But he stepped forward and shook hands with General Hernandez. "We talk in peace," Osceola said.

"Are you ready to leave Florida?" the general asked.

Once more Osceola tried to explain. The Seminoles wanted peace. They were willing to stay in the swamps white men did not need. But they did not want to leave Florida.

General Hernandez became angry. "You must promise to go at once!" he shouted.

The fever burned in Osceola's eyes. His throat was tight. He tried to speak. Then he turned to Chief Alligator. "I feel choked," he said. "You must speak for me."

As Alligator began to speak, General Hernandez waved his arm. From out of the woods, where they had been hiding, 200 mounted soldiers came at a gallop. Their guns were ready. They surrounded the Indians and seized them.

Osceola looked at General Hernandez. "Is this the way you treat the flag of truce?" his eyes seemed to say.

The general looked down. Perhaps he was ashamed of what he had done.

Because Osceola was sick, he was put on a horse. Then he and the other Indians were taken to Fort Marion.

After two months in Fort Marion, Osceola and several other chiefs were sent to Fort Moultrie near Charleston, South Carolina. Here his two wives and his small sons were allowed to join him.

To his surprise, Osceola found that he was famous. Many white people had read about his long fight for his homeland. Many of them were angry and ashamed at the way he had been captured. Well-known newspapers printed stories about him. Famous artists painted his picture.

None of this meant anything to Osceola. He longed for the dark rivers and moss-hung forests of his home. But he was too ill now to try to escape.

On the night of January 30, 1838, he could no longer speak. By a motion of his hand he told his wives to bring his best clothes. Slowly, with great effort, he got to his feet. He put on his long fringed war shirt, his leggings, and his moccasins. He buckled on his war belt with its shot pouch and powderhorn. He thrust his knife in his belt.

Osceola looked at his wives. Somehow they understood what he wanted. Quickly they brought the other Seminole chiefs. They brought the army officers of the fort. All of them stood quietly in the half-dark room, looking at Osceola.

While they watched, Osceola painted half his face and the backs of his hands with red paint. It was the sign of the warpath, the promise never to turn back. With great dignity he shook hands with the chiefs and the army officers. Gently he touched his wives and his two sons.

Now he could no longer stand. Very slowly he lay back upon his bed. With his right hand he drew the knife from his belt. Holding it, he crossed his hands on his chest. A few moments later he was dead.

After Osceola's death the Seminoles who were left in Florida continued to fight. Little by little most of them were killed or captured. At last the American army decided there were not enough Indians left to worry about. The Seminole War, the generals said, was over.

Even so, a few Seminoles remained. They made their homes deep in the Everglades. Seminoles are still in Florida today. They no longer make war against the United States. Instead, they live in peace, as Osceola had wanted. But like Osceola, they have never surrendered.

About Osceola's People

The Seminoles were runaways from the Creeks and other tribes who lived north of Florida. Together with the Chickasaws, Cherokees, Chockaws, and Creeks, the Seminoles were part of the Five Civilized Nations. They built thatch-roofed chickees to live in. They grew corn, beans, pumpkins, and squash. They hunted game and fished the lakes and rivers. The map below shows the area of the Seminole Indian War, including the Cove of the Withlacoochee, where the Seminoles won a victory; the clearing near St. Augustine, where Osceola was seized; and Fort Moultrie, where Osceola died in 1838.

Index

A

Alligator, Chief, 153
Amathla, Charley, 145, 147–148
Arpeika, 159

B

Bad Axe, Battle of the, 123, 124 (pic), 125, 126
Black Hawk, 84 (pic)
  and Black Hawk's War, 117, 118, 119, 120, 121, 122, 123–126
  childhood of, 86, 87, 88, 89, 90–93
  death of, 130
  as prisoner, 127, 128 (pic), 129
  surrender of, 127
  tours United States, 129–130
  as war chief, 96, 97, 98, 99, 100, 101 (pic), 104
  and War of 1812, 107
  and white squatters, 111–112
Black Hawk's War, 117, 118, 119, 120, 121, 122, 123–126
Blue Jacket, 61, 62, 63
Bradford, William, 35, 37, 42
Brock, Isaac, 74, 75

C

Carver, John, 27, 31, 32
Cherokee Indians, 59, 70
Chickasaw Indians, 70
Chiksika (brother of Tecumseh), 50, 51, 52, 54, 55, 56, 57, 58, 59, 60, 61
Choctaw Indians, 70
Clinch, Duncan, 153
Creek Indians, 70

D

Dade, Francis, 152
Davenport, George, 109, 110, 112, 113
Delaware Indians, 60, 63, 67

F

Fort Malden, Canada, 74, 79, 80
Fort Meigs, 76, 77
Fox Indians, 94 (pic), 95

G

Grignon, Robert, 126, 127

H

Harrison, William Henry, 67, 68, 69 (pic), 72, 76, 79
Hernandez, Joseph, 161, 162, 163
Hobomok, 20, 27, 28, 29, 33, 34, 36, 37, 38, 40

I

Indians
  Cherokee, 59, 70
  Chickasaw, 70
  Choctaw, 70
  Creek, 70
  Delaware, 60, 63, 67
  Fox, 94 (pic), 95
  Massachusetts, 20, 37
  Miami, 60, 65, 67
  Narragansett, 11, 19, 37, 38
  Osage, 94
  Pemaquid, 22
  Potawatomie, 65, 67
  Sauk, 94 (pic), 95, 99, 100, 102, 104, 105, 108, 109, 111, 112, 116, 119
  Seminole, 70, 135, 137–138, 139, 146, 152, 157, 164
  Shawnee, 50, 51, 53, 56, 60, 62, 63, 67, 82
  Sioux, 65, 94
  Wampanoag, 10, 19, 20, 22, 31, 34, 36, 40
  Winnebago, 116, 117, 119, 127
  Wyandot, 60, 65

166

S

T

W

Y